Holy Reading

Holy Reading

An Introduction to *Lectio Divina*

Innocenzo Gargano

Translated by Walter Vitale

Edited with an Introduction
by Douglas Dales

CANTERBURY
PRESS
Norwich

Translated by Walter Vitale from the Italian
Iniziazione alla Lectio Divina published
1992 by Centro Editoriale Dehoniano, Bologna.
English-language edition arranged through the
mediation of Eulama Literary Agency.

© Centro Editoriale Dehoniano, Bologna 1992

Translation © Walter Vitale 2007

Published in 2007 by the Canterbury Press Norwich
(a publishing imprint of Hymns Ancient & Modern Limited,
a registered charity)
9–17 St Alban's Place, London N1 0NX

www.scm-canterburypress.co.uk

Bible extracts are from the Revised English Bible © Oxford
University Press and Cambridge University Press 1961, 1970.

British Library Cataloguing in Publication data

A catalogue record for this book is available
from the British Library

ISBN 978-1-85311-790-9

Typeset by Regent Typesetting, London
Printed and bound by
Bookmarque, Croydon, Surrey

Contents

In grateful memory of
Pope John Paul II
and Michael Ramsey,
Archbishop of Canterbury

+

I beseech you, merciful Jesus, that as you have graciously
permitted me to drink sweetly from your Word which tells of
you, to allow me in your goodness to come at last to you, the
fountain of Wisdom, that I may stand before your face forever.

The Venerable Bede

About the author and the Camaldolese

Guido Innocenzo Gargano is a Camaldolese monk with responsibility for the spiritual and theological formation of student monks (or novices). He is prior of the monastery of San Gregorio al Celio in Rome. He has written many books of biblical theology and study, both for the specialist and for the devout laity, based on the monastic principles of *Lectio Divina*.

He also serves the Holy See in various capacities: as professor of patristic Greek theology at the Pontifical Oriental Institute, and of patristic hermeneutics at the Pontifical Biblical Institute in Rome. He has published major studies of St Gregory of Nyssa on the Song of Songs, and of patristic spirituality in the Greek and Eastern churches. He is directing the preparation of critical texts in Latin and Italian of the works of St Peter Damian, and has written studies of Camaldolese spirituality. He founded and has guided a dialogue between Jews and Christians, sponsored for 25 years by Camaldoli, and is editor of the publication *Vita Monastica*. He also has responsibility for assisting the various Oriental Christian church communities living in Rome, and fostering ecumenical meetings of those called to the monastic life in the eastern and western churches.

The Camadolese order of Benedictine monks was founded in Italy in the eleventh century by St Romuald: it comprises monks and nuns living and working in Rome and Camaldoli itself (near Arezzo), and also in Tanzania, India, Brazil and in the United States of America. The Camadolese ethos combines the community life and witness of a monastery, engaged in an active teaching programme, with the eremitic life of contemplative prayer, and an active work of mission and dialogue with modern society across the world.

Introduction

When a teacher of the Law has become a learner in the Kingdom of Heaven, he is like a householder who can produce from his store things old and new.

Matthew 13.52

This book introduces an ancient tradition of meditation on the gospel in modern dress. *Lectio Divina* is central to the Benedictine monastic way of life and it comprises learned but spiritual contemplation of the text of the Bible, as a verbal icon opening the heart and mind to Christ and to the Kingdom of Heaven. *Lectio Divina* is also central to the life of the Camaldolese monks and nuns in particular, as they open their minds to the reality of God and their hearts to those in their prayers and ministry, to whom they teach the mysteries of the gospel in this singular manner. Father Innocenzo Gargano has had long experience of both aspects of the life and witness of his order and he is also well versed in teaching the young in particular. This book therefore makes accessible the fruit of much reflection, study and prayer, drawing on a mature tradition of Christian communication and education in Italy.

This approach to the Bible speaks to the hearts and minds of many modern Christians across denominational divisions. It helps to steer a course between literalism and fundamentalism on the one hand and speculative reductionism on the other.

The tension between these two approaches has plagued biblical studies for too long, often distancing the living power of the gospel text from the minds of Christians.

The great task today is to establish an historically and linguistically consistent method of exegesis that relates the gospel text to the Greek Old Testament, the Septuagint, that was the matrix of its formation. It must also do full justice to the wisdom of the patristic and medieval monastic traditions of biblical exegesis that sustained the Church in the West until the Reformation and in the East until today, while benefiting from more modern critical historical and textual approaches. Upon this basis it should be possible to bring together the spiritual and the ethical implications of the gospel, seen in the light of the rest of the Bible. Only then will the Church be able, in the words of the late Pope John Paul II, 'to breathe with both its lungs', eastern and western, and to communicate the life-giving power of the gospel of Christ with full and effective authority to modern society. In so doing the Church will discover another dimension of its inherent unity, across the world and throughout the ages, by coming closer through the Bible to Christ who is the living Word of God.

The roots of this book lie in two lovely and holy places at the heart of Italian Catholic Christianity. Camaldoli lies high in the mountains of Tuscany, in the forests of the Casentino above Poppi near Arezzo. Founded almost one thousand years ago as a colony of hermits under the spiritual leadership of St Romuald, it has persisted in faithful prayer and monastic witness through many interesting and sometimes turbulent centuries. It has maintained close links with eastern Christianity since before the Great Schism, and was also influential in the theology and learning of the early Renaissance in Florence. Today it is the mother house of a family of monasteries for men and women in Italy and in

Rome itself, and also in America, Tanzania, Brazil and India. Its horizons are global while its heart is strictly contemplative. The hermitages remain enclosed within an encircling wall, amidst towering trees and high up on the mountain above the monastery itself. It remains a centre of ecumenical hospitality and Christian teaching, faithful in its ethos to the memory of one of its great friends, Cardinal Montini, who became Pope Paul VI.

Father Innocenzo Gargano works in Rome, as a teaching professor and servant of the Catholic Church in the city, as a mentor to student monks from across the world, and as the prior of the ancient and lovely monastery of San Gregorio al Celio. This is the monastery founded by Pope St Gregory the Great in his own home, from which St Augustine and his monks came to bring Christianity to England in AD 597. It lies in the heart of Rome, opposite the Palatine hill and above the Circus Maximus. It is surrounded by some most beautiful and interesting old churches and is not far from the city walls and the Via Appia that leads out to the catacombs. The aegis of St Gregory hovers over the place where he prayed, which is still identified in a side chapel replete with his marble chair. It is certainly appropriate and moving that his monastery should be in the care of the Camadolese, who in their Benedictine ethos preserve the blend of education, contemplation and mission that marked the monastically led church of the Anglo-Saxons, which St Gregory initiated and nurtured over many centuries by his teaching and prayers.

It has been a great privilege and pleasure to edit this book for publication in English and so to be able to repay in a small measure the generous kindness and hospitality that Father Innocenzo and his community have always shown to my wife and myself and to our children on our several visits to San Gregorio and Camaldoli in recent years. The dedication of this book reflects a happy collaboration between a Catholic and an Anglican, united in love for the Word of God.

Douglas Dales, Marlborough
Candlemas, 2006

I

Introducing *Lectio Divina*

We propose in these pages an initiation into *Lectio Divina*, as it has been practised by many Benedictine monks and nuns, following a methodology that goes back for the most part to the fathers of the Church, with the addition of some elements that owe a debt to modern biblical exegesis.

There are many ways of reading the Bible: sometimes reading it out of simple curiosity for the history of the religion that gave it birth, that is, either Hebrew or Christian history; or for strictly philological interest, in order to clarify the literal meaning of the text by academic study and by exegetical research. The way of reading the Bible called *Lectio Divina* does not exclude these other approaches, it presupposes them and is indeed complementary to them; but its specific purpose is to bring us to prayer and to contemplation.

Sustained reflection on *Lectio Divina* and its practice has been particularly developed in some monastic traditions. According to one of them, the Benedictine tradition, Christian monks and nuns see in the Scriptures a lively organism, almost a person that engages us. When meeting with a person we pose questions and expect answers; we do the same with the Scriptures, considering them to be in some way alive, so that the answers that we are given are always those addressed to living people. Our relationship with the Scriptures is of a personal nature: it means being actively involved and not abstracted or divorced by a detached or 'scientific' spirit. Consequently the more we bind our own spiritual history and our very selves to them, the more we believe we can comprehend their deeper significance, their inner soul. According to biblical understanding, the deepest knowledge of a person is obtained when one unites with another person, in the measure by which I become, let us say, of one kin with someone else, putting myself into the thoughts and worries of that other person, sharing in their very life: then I arrive at deeper comprehension of the other.

This kind of knowledge, through a kind of affinity that is based, according to the language of Thomist theology, on our common humanity, is in fact an ancient principle of research into the truth, already expressed by the ancient philosophers in the axiom that 'only the same knows the same'. Following this principle, conformity to the spirit of the Scriptures is the main path to their comprehension, because conformity to Christ is the true road to knowledge of him.

There is however no mutual exclusion between the two principles, of scientific research and what we could describe as wisdom searching for the truth: they in fact complement each other. The sense of affinity must be developed first through sensitivity to the actual letter of the Scripture, which is in fact the first object of any exegetical research. Referring to the mystery of Christ the Incarnate Word, there is the axiom *cardo salutis caro*: the cardinal point of salvation is in the flesh of Christ. This is valid also in relation to Scripture: the meaning of the visible word, which we reach through the technical help of exegetical experts, becomes the basis for deeper knowledge of Christ, and of the personal relationship that will be established with him.

The literal sense is therefore the basis, the objective fact, to clarify which we need the help of scientific and historical exegesis. But, once it is clarified, it is necessary to go beyond, because authentic knowledge of the truth can only be achieved through loving participation in it. It is this last element that characterizes the monastic tradition of reading the Scripture. Introducing the monastic journey, the *Rule of Saint Benedict* speaks of the Scripture as the voice of a living person. Thus in the prologue to his *Rule* St Benedict says:

> Our eyes wide open to the divine light, our ears alerted, let us hearken to the voice of God which warns us every day: 'O that today you would hearken to his voice! Harden not your hearts.' . . . What could be more delightful than this invitation of our Lord, dear brothers? See how in his fatherly kindness the Lord points out to us the way of life. So then, our loins girt with faith and the practice of good works, let us travel along His ways under the guidance of the gospel, so that we may deserve to see Him who has called us into His kingdom.

It is necessary to be convinced that the deepest dimension of the Scriptures is the voice of the Lord Jesus Christ, the Word of God, in order to be able to catch its deeper meaning: for Scripture is not just any book. Origen said that the words of love that the bridegroom, Jesus, exchanges with his bride the Church become witnesses to a loving exchange: the hearing of the words of Scripture has the object of involving us in the very depths of our being, because it is to us that these words are directed. The 'divine voice', 'the voice of the Lord', 'the love of the gospel' must be the constant reference points for those who want to enter into what St Benedict calls *'dominici schola servitii'*, 'a school of the Lord's service'. A person enters a community, a monastery, because in it the Lord speaks, and He speaks through the words of Holy Scripture. There are no other words of direction. Even when the Abbot expresses an order, it must be compared with the word of the gospel, which the Abbot himself must first obey.

I love to read a text that does not belong to the monastic tradition, however, but to the Hebrew rabbinical tradition that was absorbed by the first Church fathers, and which has become a fundamental point of reference for entire ages of monastic tradition. This text gives some background in depth to the kind of *Lectio Divina* that we want to present. Its editorial production goes back to around AD 1300, but it has behind it a tradition that is centuries old.

The Torah, which is for the rabbis the heart of Holy Scripture, reveals a Word that emerges from its veil and then hides itself again. She acts like this only with those who know her and are obedient to her. The Torah in fact looks like a beautiful and magnificent girl, hidden in a remote room of her palace. She has a secret love, unknown to all others. The one in love with her for the love of her looks attentively through the lattice of the house in each direction, searching for her. She knows that her beloved insists on frequenting the windows of the house, so what does she do? She opens the door of her remote room just a bit, and for an instant reveals her face to the beloved, but then hides it again. Anyone in the company of the beloved would neither see nor perceive anything. Only the beloved sees her, and he is dragged inwardly towards her with his heart and soul, indeed with all his being. He understands that for the love of him she has disclosed herself for an instant, inflamed by love for him. Such is the Word of the Torah that reveals herself only to those truly beloved. So the Torah reveals and at the same time hides herself, and is inebriated with love for the beloved, while stimulating love within him.

Come and see how this is the way of the Torah. At the

beginning when she wants to reveal herself to someone, she offers only a sudden sign. If a person does not understand, she insists and calls with a thin kind of voice. To the messenger sent by her, the Torah says: 'Tell the one who is able to perceive this little voice, to come here because then I can talk to him; for it is written: One who is simple comes to me.' She thus speaks and desires that he understands.

When he comes to her, she starts to address to him in clearer words from behind the veil, educating him to comprehend, until very slowly there is conceived and born within him a spiritual intuition. Then, through a veil of light, she transmits to him allegorical words. It is only then, when he has become familiar to her, that she reveals herself face to face, and speaks to him of all the hidden mysteries and of all the roads to follow that she had in her heart to tell him from the beginning. A person of this kind is then called perfect and becomes a spiritual master. That is like saying a 'Bridegroom of the Torah' in the most intimate and precise sense; for that person becomes the master of the house, to whom she opens all her secrets, not hiding anything from him. She tells him: 'You see now how many mysteries the simple signs I gave you on that first day contained, and what was their true meaning?' Then he understands that to those words nothing can be taken away or added; and he comprehends, for the first time, the meaning of the Word of the Torah, as if it were there in front of him: words to which not a syllable or a consonant can be added or subtracted.

Zohar, Mishpatim 99a–99b

This text exposes with great clarity the relationship that must be established with Holy Scripture if we wish to reach a deeper knowledge. Scientific-exegetical knowledge reveals in this context its limitations and relativity: for by remaining caged within it, even though it remains the basis for study, a person would end up not grasping the deeper meaning of Scripture, which we identify with the mystery of God; yet it is towards this mystery that *Lectio Divina* must reach out.

Sensitive respect for the Word of God, and recognition that nothing can be added to or subtracted from Holy Scripture, must be reiterated and stressed: for it reveals that in each word, even the most insignificant, can hide divine mystery. This method of approach corresponds to that of the Church fathers and also to the teaching of Jesus, who affirms that: 'Not a letter, not a dot, will disappear from the Law (Torah) until all that must happen has happened' (Matthew 5.18).

In this way the initial literal reading, typical of the *Lectio Divina,* becomes a deep hearing of the Word of God, a hearing that can occur only in silence and in solitude, those unique spaces in which the small voice of the Scripture becomes audible. We must in some way, in other words, relive the experience of Elijah on the holy mountain, who needed to sharpen his own ear before discovering the voice of the Lord inside 'a gentle murmuring wind' (1 Kings 19.9–14).

According to St Benedict, a monk sharpens his sense of hearing through prayer, dedicating it as far as possible to the Word of God. In the *Rule of Saint Benedict* there is prescribed a determined and definite measure of time to be given daily to *Lectio Divina.* Thus monasteries become locations for listening to the Word of God. Also their location and often their geographical solitude, and the physical silence pursued as a rule of life, enable within a monk that transformation into a silence that is more inwardly oriented and attuned to this kind of hearing. The Scriptures themselves, as they become more familiar, educate a person into this inward silence and spiritual journey.

6

2

Foundations for *Lectio Divina*

In the thinking of the fathers and of the monastic tradition, the preparation of an inner spiritual space, adequate for the kind of hearing that characterizes *Lectio Divina,* rests upon certain general assumptions that are common to all Christians.

Faith

The first assumption that makes possible *Lectio Divina* is faith. When monks or nuns take in their hands the books of Scripture they start from an attitude of faith: they believe that God has inspired the Bible.

What does it mean to believe that the Bible is inspired? It means that, when a holy writer writes, the Holy Spirit protects him from writing errors regarding faith itself. But for monks and nuns it also means, according to the teaching of Origen, that the Holy Spirit is present in the Scriptures. Scripture is seen in a similar way to how a Christian believer sees the Eucharist: under the veil of the bread and wine there is truly present the resurrected One; so the monk or nun is convinced that under the veil of the words of Holy Scripture the Holy Spirit is present. Obviously this is not a presence that excludes other presences of the Spirit, just as the presence of Jesus in the Eucharist does not exclude his presence elsewhere. The Second

Vatican Council speaks of the real presence of the Lord also in the sick, in the community, in the hierarchy that transmits the teaching of the apostles, and in many other situations; for as the Lord promises: 'where two or three meet together in my name, I am there among them' (Matthew 18.20).

The presence of the Holy Spirit in the Scriptures is therefore a real presence. In the monastic context it is usual to find two lamps lit: one facing the Holiest One and the other facing the book of the Holy Scriptures. There is an awareness that the Spirit moves in the Scriptures; he is really present in the Scriptures. The liturgy permits us to adopt towards the Scriptures an unequivocal attitude of veneration, expressed by the offering of incense, and in the kiss. To open oneself to the books of the Scriptures means to let oneself be enlightened by the light of the Holy Spirit that inspired them and who is present within them.

The unity of the two testaments in the Easter mystery of Christ

A second assumption underlying the understanding of *Lectio Divina* that we propose is the unity of the two parts of Scripture. The same Spirit that has inspired the New Testament has inspired the Old Testament. This seems an obvious affirmation, almost unnecessary. But it is actually a very important assumption, because in referring to the Old Testament we are referring to God the creator, who in Genesis 1 not only made all things, but has Himself an attitude of contemplation towards each creature, affirming that everything is beautiful or 'good', and even more emphatically about human nature being 'very good'. This implies that God the redeemer of the New Testament cannot have given to us redemption radically different from the act of creation itself. The tradition that says that grace presupposes nature means, we could say, that grace presupposes the creature: for if there is no recipient, there is no receiving of grace. If one does not accept the creation in its visible reality, one cannot speak of its invisible spiritual manifestation. This is the fundamental criterion for understanding the Incarnation of the Word of God: to be able to reach and come to faith in the Son of God, we must start by recognizing the Son of Mary, Jesus of Nazareth, in his humanity as the Messiah and Lord.

We must now move forward in our thinking. Obviously in our spiritual experience these two aspects, the visible and invisible, present themselves within the unfolding of the temporal order as we experience it, because we only see wholeness in a single moment. But there is always the need to be aware of another succession within reality that is both rational and ideal. For if we eliminate humanity, we eliminate creation: in which case we would have neither the Christian, nor the new creation – that creation which we see transfigured and transformed in the redemption of Jesus Christ. This means that whatever dualism, division or conflict between that which is visible and tangible, which we identify with the flesh, and that which is invisible and intangible, which we identify with the spirit, cannot be a Christian concept. The unity of the two testaments means that it is God's own Spirit revealing Himself through the facts, the characters, the words and the correspondences between them. He is the continuous bond of attachment among them.

This obviously means a positive vision of the world and of human history: it is a vision that asserts that all that belongs to the history of humanity contains a message that comes from the Lord. It implies that the more we are able to perceive this, the more we will let ourselves be enlightened by that light, which for us is the presence of the Son of God in the person of

Jesus of Nazareth. (John 1.1–9) It follows that we illuminate the Old and the New Testaments in the light of the death and resurrection of Jesus. As the fathers say, we highlight the shadows and we distinguish them from the truth. In Christ, we can begin to discern between the fallen word, which would threaten to kill us spiritually if we were to fix ourselves upon it, and the Spirit, which regenerates and continuously opens us to the renewing Word of God. Our encounter with the central mystery of the death and resurrection of Jesus is the criteria of discernment that allows us to move from the letter of the word to the spirit of the truth of both Testaments. The light of the Paschal mystery of Jesus allows us to go beyond all obstacles, all the partialities, deficiencies and restrictions of the cultural contexts that are present in the Old as well as in the New Testament.

For it is easy enough to find in the Old Testament situations that are apparently incomprehensible and unacceptable for any Christian vision: acts of violence, cursing, etc. Similar situations also occur in the New Testament, for example the anti-Jewish polemic in John's Gospel, or in Matthew 23, some expressions in the Acts of the Apostles, the violence expressed in the Apocalypse, the cultural conditioning of Paul. The necessary principle of discernment for handling all these texts remains comparison with the death and resurrection of Jesus of Nazareth. This means that any affirmation, contained in the words of the two Testaments, that would put in parenthesis this mystery, or that would preclude the full manifestation of the consequences of the death and resurrection of Christ, could never be the ultimate meaning of that expression in Scripture desired by the Lord for our community, for the Church and for each one of us. To keep these principles in mind will help us a great deal when we encounter texts, situations or characters in the Bible that could leave us perplexed.

Communion with the Church

A third indispensable assumption underlying *Lectio Divina* is communion with the Church. The Church constitutes the horizontal dimension, the physical manifestation of its own Easter mystery of Jesus in whom, by the presence of the one Spirit, the unity of the two Testaments is created.

Christians must be aware that the Church community offers Scripture to us: it is a treasure that is put in our hands in a living manner by a living community. The books of Scripture are not a self-centred or self-enclosed world of discovery. It may happen that someone may get closer to them on their own; but the body of the Scriptures will bring that person inevitably to a community that makes of this book its vital reference point. Any self-centred encounter is not sufficient, for as the ancient fathers used to say: *'Ecclesia tenet et legit librum scripturarum'* (It is the Church that keeps and reads the books of the Scriptures).

This means that if you are not part of the Church you cannot claim ownership of the Scriptures, and much less can you pretend to be able to read them fully. It means that to encounter and have access in depth to understanding of Scripture, it is necessary to be in communion with the Church, which is the particular community that gathers in the name of Jesus, but is also the community that expands to the very boundaries of the world. It is not enough, therefore, to establish a peaceful relationship just between two or three fellow Christians, because this would be again risky: it could open the way to a closed group form of individualism, shut in on itself. Communion, however, by its very nature obliges openness: closed communities cannot encapsulate the Scriptures. Only communities that allow themselves to be led by the Holy Spirit are truly open.

Scripture is, in fact, the treasure of Christ hidden within the domain of the Church. When the importance and value of this treasure is perceived, there arises the courage to sell everything to buy this land. To sell all is to become a part of the Church wherein this treasure is buried. To be able to enter into the ecclesial communion where there is this possibility of discovering the treasure hidden in Holy Scripture, it is however necessary to have the courage to sell all, to consider the rest of life disposable, as St Paul says. All the surrogates that have been depended upon like crutches in order to arrive at an encounter with the Word of God – these we must have the courage to throw away, even though it is very difficult to rely on the Word of God, risking as it seems a fall into the void.

If Scripture is read in the community of the Church, it must be read in the wholeness of communion within the life of the Church. Even if this is the highest goal, it cannot pretend to monopolize the Church, however, or to be the synthesis of all the gifts of the Spirit, or to possess all his charisms. No, each person has a particular gift and the Spirit alone has the gift of synthesis; nobody has all his gifts, because the Holy Spirit distributes the gifts as he pleases.

St Benedict used to say that no one must be excluded from being regarded as a recipient of the Spirit, because very often the Holy Spirit reveals himself to the least in the community, indicating to the smallest and least considered member something which is necessary and useful for the regeneration of the whole community. Whoever closes himself or herself to the revelation of the Spirit, by being closed to the enrichment of faith that may indeed come from the least in the community, cannot pretend to be in communion with the Catholic and inclusive spirit of the Church.

The ancient fathers did not conceive of a Church that was stagnantly subdivided: the development of Catholic monasti-

FOUNDATIONS FOR *LECTIO DIVINA*

cism was rather intended in the most dynamic and active sense possible. Its vocation is to reiterate all that the Church is meant to be. Thus all those who are searching for the deeper meaning of Holy Scripture must first of all be concerned to be in communion with other members of the mysterious Body of Christ, with all the other members of the Church. The authentic Body of Christ is the whole community of the Church, which is born and finds itself again within the mystery of gathering around the Eucharist. For the ancient fathers the mystical Body of Christ was found in the Eucharist, whose reality is indeed the community of the Church. There is no conflict between these two presences of Christ: for the presence of Jesus in the Eucharist is his presence in the sacramental mystery under the veil of the bread and the wine; while the Body of Christ, which constitutes the presence of Jesus resurrected in history, comprises all Christian believers. We are members, says St Paul, of this one Body and we all have one head, Jesus Christ our Lord.

Continuous conversion

The ancient fathers used to speak about the possibility of continuous conversion that is required by *Lectio Divina* (and we reiterate it): that it is impossible to comprehend the books of the Scriptures if a person is not willing to renounce a merely horizontal vision, comprising pretensions to self-sufficiency and reliance upon intellectual wealth, or personal preoccupation with everyday life. Instead these must be replaced by dependence on the Word of God. It may be possible to read the Bible on the surface, but if there is no willingness to put ourselves under review, including our own certainties, wealth, and self-sufficiencies, the holy book will remain closed, even though it may materially appear open in front of us. It is necessary first to divest the dispositions of our own hearts so that the Word of God can evangelize us afresh with his divine richness.

In this process of conversion is bound up all the perception and ascetic effort of monastic communities. Ultimately, what is the commitment of a monastic community if not the effort to purify the heart, through the emptying of the mind of all that is superfluous, in order to be fulfilled by the Word of God? The Catholic monk or nun, from morning to evening and also in the night, following obediently the abbot's fatherly direction and discipline, becomes reverently orientated by the Holy Spirit, to allow himself or herself to be completely impregnated by the Word of God, until the moment of dawn, in which that person will become inwardly transfigured by Christ the Word of God.

The message of the monks that relates to the Christian life is this: in the measure by which a Christian becomes capable of conversion to Christ, in the same measure Christ reveals himself to them. There is a parallel in what Jesus used to say about forgiveness: if you forgive, it will be forgiven to you. Here it may be said: if you will bend towards the Scripture, towards the Word of God, the Word of God will bend towards you. There needs to be a reciprocal act and disposition of condescension. If you bend, the other also bends to you; if you remain rigid, the other also remains rigid. Let us have always in our vision a loving relationship. Indeed, the Word of God is so free and awake, as the fathers say, as to make himself a child with children, young with the youthful, adult with adults, thus making each to understand things that correspond to the level of their inward journey. This is the progression of knowledge and of intimations of eternal life, which derive from the search for God through the Scriptures.

If we are stagnant in our religious moralism, the Word of

God will tell us only so much and no more. But if we have the courage to go beyond, the Word will also go beyond towards us. Jesus respects the growth of each of us, and reveals himself in the measure by which we are capable and willing to welcome him. These are signs of the maternal tenderness of the Word of God. For a mother knows how to endure the nine months of gestation, and knows how to match appropriate food to each age of her children.

The gift of the Holy Spirit through prayer

There is another indispensable assumption: in order to be able to catch the deeper sense of the Scripture in this mode of reading and of seeking divine wisdom through *Lectio Divina*, the gift of the Holy Spirit is needed as the fathers teach. We know that it is the Spirit who has inspired the Scriptures: he is contained in the Scriptures, and it is the Spirit that knows the depths of God. Who therefore can pretend to penetrate the depths of the Spirit, if the Spirit himself does not initiate them? We could use all the techniques that we wanted; we could also commit ourselves very intensively to a level of moral discipline: but without the gift of the Holy Spirit the books of the Scriptures remain closed before us. No techniques, no *ascesis* of itself can reveal it to us: the deep sense of the Holy Scripture is a secret that only the Spirit knows; and he reveals it to whom he wills, how and where and when he wants: 'The wind blows where it wills: you hear the sound of it, but you do not know where it comes from or where it is going' (John 3.8).

This affirmation is sufficient to cause all our human pretensions to fall. If the Spirit gives us this gift, we come to know the things of the Spirit; but if he does not give it to us, we do not know them. It is a gift and as such it is not an obligation; it is by definition free. A person would achieve only despair who would try to force the Spirit to come: for the Spirit does not allow himself to be forced. It is necessary to ask further about this inner journey that the Church fathers would have us make. It is necessary to ask insistently for the gift of the Spirit, and this must be asked for in the name of Jesus, who guarantees the welcoming of our prayer by the Father. Only prayer made in the name of Jesus and in communion with fellow Christians will in fact be fulfilled. For the gospel of Matthew says: 'If two of you agree on earth about any request you have to make, that request will be granted by my heavenly Father' (Matthew 18.19).

Self-centred invocation is not enough: it must be the fruit of harmony lived in community. St Jerome says that the Lord hears only those prayers that are born from harmony lived within a community of brethren. Where there is no harmony, there is no authentic call of the Spirit. His call cannot be heard because the Spirit speaks always to the community, through the community and within the community. Only when we become together a genuine voice of the Spirit, will the Spirit welcome us, because it is the Spirit who rushes to our call, and who is himself the object of our call. To catch the deep sense of the Scripture we need, in the end, the gift of true prayer; but we understand that this prayer is only authentic and capable of being fulfilled by the Father if it starts from harmony lived within a Christian community, offering itself in the name of the Lord.

Very early in the Greek monastic tradition, which is the most ancient one, there was the axiom that when finally we are able to pray – and we have seen now what authentic Christian prayer means – do we reach also the experience of theology. An ancient father of the Church, Evagrius Pontus, used to say: 'if you pray truly, you are a theologian; and it will only be possible to claim to be a theologian when we have learned truly to pray'. Prayer invokes the Holy Spirit of which Jesus says: 'He will guide you into all the truth' (John 16.13). Without the gift of the Spirit the truth remains far from us, because it is itself the mystery of God, contained within the deep mystery of the Scriptures: this is the living theology that we want our life to become through *Lectio Divina*. We do not come to the mystery of God the Father except through the truth revealed in the Son. But the Son is only revealed to us in the Spirit; and the Spirit is not given to us apart from the communion of the Church: this is the pattern of connections that underlies *Lectio Divina*.

3

The ascetic study of Scripture

We have seen how many are the inner spiritual attitudes necessary for *Lectio Divina*. It is appropriate now to add that our daily *ascesis*, our personal struggle as a Christian, can be and indeed in some measure must be constructed around the Holy Scriptures, and our commitment to growth must be orientated by hearing the Word of God. Silence, as we have seen, enables hearing; equally important also is stability of life, which entails a similar permanent commitment to continuous conversion and a keen awareness of never having reached any goal by ourselves. The same is true for the solitude of the monastic cell. If these three characteristics of the monastic life, and of the religious life in general, do not enable true hearing to develop that is sensitive to the depths of Scripture and to the centrality of the Word of Christ in our life, they become in-effectual; and we know that what is ineffectual often becomes the source of vice.

We can and may follow spiritual and ascetic directions that come to us from other religions and places; but such teachings must be tested for their relative truth by our encounter with the Word of God. Certainly other spiritual traditions have their own strength and usefulness, but only in so far as they do not constitute a barrier between the Word of God and us. Instead, by leading us by the hand, as it were, they should bring us towards him. If this is not so, it is necessary to have the courage to let go of the most precious support on which we may have built our own spiritual life. It is very difficult to do this, but we must make the Word of God, the only begotten One, the Lord of our life. Otherwise we will always be walking in ambiguity. It is a bit like wanting to remain behind to bury one's own father (cf. Matthew 8.21), being always about to do something, but in reality never deciding to make Christ and his Word the absolute foundation of our lives.

The study of Holy Scripture has been for many generations of monks and nuns the first duty in the true, personal, daily hard commitment of spiritual *ascesis*. Let us think of St Jerome, the great biblical teacher of the western Church: any monk that is able to sit for eight hours a day at his table to read and study the Scripture is indeed an ascetic, even if he eats meat and does not observe practices that are deemed regular in a monastic community. If he has constancy in the study of the Scriptures his is indeed an authentic monastic or religious *ascesis*.

First of all then, study of the letter of the Scripture is necessary, without any shortcuts or detours toward spiritual fruition; for this would deny the discovery that the literal meaning of the Scripture is already spiritual nourishment for the soul. Certainty that the literal meaning is already its own kind of spiritual nourishment, and that the hard work it entails is a true *ascesis*, induces us to use all means to attain accurate comprehension of the text. Accepting with humility the need to learn the a-b-c of reading and comprehension of a text, often in a foreign language, is a spiritual commitment: it is obedience in all due diligence towards the Word of God. The reliability of such research requires the necessary discipline and constancy that we must show to attain authentic *Lectio Divina*. For if the basics are not well established, the result of our reading will be simply a fantasy, self indulgent and shallowly spiritual, whereby the Word of God, instead of being the Lord of our life, becomes the servant of our temporal and often temporary feelings.

Some monastic-ascetic methodologies

The monastic tradition knows also about an *ascesis* that stays close to understanding the letter of the Scripture, a methodology all of its own. For example, St Romuald submitted for three years to a spiritual master, called Marino, who taught him nothing else than to read attentively the book of the psalms. According to St Romuald the essential path of the spiritual journey for a monk is traceable in the psalms.

At the monastery of Fontavellana, in the Italian province of Marche, there is a beautiful room called the scriptorium, with two ranks of windows because the light had to be very clear inside the room as in it the monks transcribed their texts. It was the constant rule in the monasteries that the first text to transcribe for beginners would always be the book of the Holy Scriptures. When they had demonstrated their knowledge of how to transcribe the literal text with attention, only then could they advance.

To memorize, to read with awareness and wholeheartedly, and to transcribe the text are three very simple modes of operation, within the reach of everybody, beginning the journey of *Lectio Divina*. This could only be done in a determined location, however, and in a prescribed way, under the alert and paternal eye of the abbot.

If we accept the natural presupposition that every type of human activity should be fulfilled with attention, concentrating the eyes of the mind without distraction, then we are confronted by the twofold state of mind in the monastery of wakefulness and fasting. Fasting does not mean simply not eating: it means not to over burden ourselves during meals; for there should always be an opportunity to get up from the table with a bit of an appetite. This is the measure of fasting, because only in such a way is it possible to become aware physically and with the eyes of the mind awakened, giving full attention to the Word of God. This should be the context in which our experience of *Lectio Divina* occurs.

The sayings of the fathers are fully aware of the risks that are taken when certain forms of *ascesis*, like those of wakefulness and fasting, are united together as an experience in itself, without being accompanied by that constant and searching purity of heart that will allow us clearly to see in the words of the Scripture the Word of God. Careful eyes of the mind must accompany purity of the heart, because Jesus in the gospel has explicitly affirmed the blessedness of those who are pure in heart, for they will see God.

It is clear then that external *ascesis*, or a merely external attitude, would not be of any use if unaccompanied by this continuous purification of the heart, which is the indispensable foundation of *Lectio Divina*. The monastic fathers attained extreme acuteness in analysing the causes of inattention among monks in their first phase of commitment to *Lectio Divina*. Evagrius of Pontus, a great monk of the desert at the end of the fourth century, indicates the eight deadly sins and their accompanying temptations as the distractions monks often experience during *Lectio Divina*, as the great enemies of the attention of the heart. It is therefore vital that the heart is purified, so that the eye of the mind becomes aware of the Word of God.

Philological techniques

The ancient fathers knew that it is not enough simply by superficial reading to catch the meaning of Scripture. On the one hand the spiritual master, who was always present, contributed suggestions drawn from his own experience conducive for the progressive purification of the heart; on the other hand, commitment on the part of the monk was necessary to tread in the most intensive way possible the pages of Scripture in order to press the juice like wine from grapes. For this treading of the text, particular techniques existed that varied according to the diversity of the books of Scripture in their literal forms. These are techniques already present in the great philologists and commentators of the Hellenistic and Mediterranean world, for the fathers were steeped in the intellectual culture of their day. They are not far removed from the study of grammar in school today.

Grammatical analysis

The term 'grammar' comes from *gramma*, which means 'letter': each letter is weighed and defined, because each single letter and term has its own particular quality. This is particularly true with reference to the Hebrew language, where each word is also a symbol: so to be aware of the letter means also to have the eye opened to the mysterious dimension that hides behind the letter. A comparable argument could also be made pertaining to the letters of our alphabet, which derive from Greek and the Latin.

Beyond having symbolic function, the letters of the Hebrew and Greek alphabets have also a numerical value. This could be expressed through the letters so that each word referred to mysterious realities that transcended the letters themselves. In the New Testament there are various examples of this kind. Sometimes a number, for example five or seven, appears: five thousand people, 153 great fish, etc. (cf. John 21.11) These are amounts that have a mysterious significance that we must try to elucidate.

In this kind of grammatical analysis, attention is given to the letter of the text in the most precise sense of the term – the letter of the alphabet. By this 'attention to the letter' we take note also of the word 'vocabulary'. For each piece of vocabulary has its own identity. To discover it is indispensable for any comprehension of the text. Each word of vocabulary is in fact the fruit of an initial root, which, through the transposition of letters, insertion of vowels, addition of prefixes or suffixes, gives a determinate body of meaning. By concentrating for a moment on this term and analysing it as such, we already encounter in some way an infinite field of potential meanings. We next have to consider the position that words have inside a phrase. It could be a verb that then points towards a certain meaning; or it could be an adverb, an adjective, etc. Beyond taking into consideration what constitutes the term, we need to be aware of its own quality or presence inside a phrase.

This approach is useful, and not too difficult, and it is the first attentive technique used when reading a text. The careful reader cannot afford to forget the specific nature of the single chain of words with which each affirmation in the text is textured. Indeed a texture cannot be created except through diverse chains of words. Once these chains have been identified in a single range of vocabulary, the further step is that of understanding how these vocabularies are interwoven, constructing the texture, and making their identity accessible. The chains of words within a texture always go beyond its own border: in this sense, once having identified a chain of meaning, we can in some way follow it towards an infinite perspective. Generally this analysis involves going in search of the verb. There is always one chain that is more important than the others, because that is what unifies the rest. It acts as a kind of common denominator that must be participated in by everybody; otherwise the texture breaks. This driving force, that draws all together, is in general the verb: for it is the verb that connects words. Without the verb we do not know what the relationship is between nouns, adjectives and adverbs.

Logical analysis

The discovery of the verb opens the way to the next step of logical analysis: the rationale and consequential nature of a phrase. Terms are interwoven according to a logical connection. Through this kind of analysis, we may search to discover this rationale. So nouns start to define themselves as subject and object and so on. This analysis reveals the sequence existing in the construction of a proposition.

In this analysis we discover in larger passages what is the principal affirmation that the author intends. Once discovered, we begin to see all the coordinates, the subordinates, and certain incidental phrases, apparently insignificant, but now giving the tone and not just the frame, adding colour to the rest of the argument. Having highlighted with transparency the structure of the writing and its own central affirmation, we alight on the subject, the predicate, and the various components of the principal proposition, forgetting for an instant all the rest.

Then we concentrate on the verb, probing it; we examine it critically, with patience and repeatedly, to understand its meaning fully. From the philological point of view we uncover first of all the root of the verb in order to catch its 'radical' sense, and to discover the multiple shades of meaning that arise from the entire range of derivatives from the same common root. A root can give poignancy to the formation of a verb, or of a noun, an adjective, or an adverb. Let us think for example of the verb 'to love': the same root gives origin to the words 'love', 'lovely', 'lover', etc. It is very useful to keep in mind the root, because it gives us the possibility of moving spaciously around it.

This search is full of fruits for those who have the possibility of tapping into the roots of one of the two original languages of the Scriptures, Greek and Hebrew. Others will be able to press the words with a simpler mode of engagement, searching, for example, with the help of a good dictionary, for synonyms and antonyms, and broadening their inquiry into the range of meaning implied with the addition or the subtraction of a determining prefix, suffix, or whatever. Even without knowledge of Greek or Latin, we have the possibility to investigate a term. Think again of the verb 'to love': each one of us is able to say the same thing with some other synonym. Our synonyms may have a little idiosyncrasy, but each one will show a diverse cut of the crystal we have in our hand. The more we turn it around, the more we discover colours that we did not think were present.

Take for example the verb 'to reveal', which is very frequently used in the Bible. We have three synonyms in the words 'reveal', 'clarify' and 'to manifest'. If we use the word 'reveal' we give the sense of a veil taken away, of a secret revealed. If we use instead the word 'to manifest' we accentuate the appearance of something, its 'epiphany'. If we take away the prefix 're-' from 'reveal' we have the opposite, 'to veil', in other words to close, to conceal, to hide, to cover, to obscure. This analysis helps us to understand the sense of the term 'to reveal', chosen here as an example. Often to understand better the pregnancy of an antonym or of a synonym, we need to construct a phrase with it, so that the term clarifies itself more and more. By this elementary engagement we can catch the pregnancy of meaning that hides inside the form of a definite word and slowly we will become aware that our *Lectio Divina* is starting to bear fruit. Thus we press a word while we are still at the level of careful reading of the text. This is not the preserve of an expert: what is needed is only persistent humility and fidelity.

Structural analysis

We have spoken until now of a progressive pattern of grammatical analysis and logic, examining the structure of words, respecting their order and the gradual nature of these modes of analysis. Now let us take a more particular approach.

Let us search to discover the most adequate structure of a text, without presupposing that this is the only possible one: in fact, our structural analysis is often determined by a certain anticipation. We interpose our own preconceptions upon a page, and obviously the structure that emerges from it tends to answer to these subjective preconceptions. Let us demonstrate the utmost respect towards the text; but let us not delude ourselves that our structure is the only possible one. Beyond the risk of preconception remains the fact that the Bible evinces many and multiple constructions of a text. It is not written according to an imposed unity, and each part has to be analysed in a particular way; because the structure of a part does not necessarily correspond to that of another part, even if it comes immediately next.

Biblical exegetes as academic technicians have given us

certain parameters of reference; one thinks of the work of Jeremias on the common structure of the parables. Other exegetes have indicated to us the structure of a story or a miracle. Then there are the structures regarding various stories that are neither parables nor miracles: these are the *logia*, the sayings of the Lord and the constructions around them. There are also structures that reflect catechetical preoccupations, or even hint at liturgical initiation. All of these have to be kept in mind each time we face a page of the gospel, because one of these structures or paradigms can be present within it.

The complexity of such structural analysis must not alarm us. We wish to reach through *Lectio Divina* an experience of prayer in the deepest possible way: this is what counts and is important. The ancient monks sought this: for them it was enough to know how to read and write; even more it was enough to be able to retain something in the memory. Sometimes then the ancient spiritual fathers synthesized the body of the Word of God in short written maxims, which summarized in the end the entire Scripture. These maxims became ejaculatory in prayer, and were used by the monks like burning javelins against their spiritual enemies. This demonstrates how important the spiritual journey indicated by Scripture was and is, into which a person enters with the means that each has available, be it the most simple, seeking only the reward of its inner message.

Let us examine anyway the simplest forms of structure of the biblical pages, seeking how to utilize them for our own spiritual journey. We all know how to distinguish within the story of a miracle in the gospel the initial moment in which a problematic situation is presented by an individual or a specific group; then the central moment constituted by the decisive encounter with the person of Jesus; followed by a word of his or a sign by him that constitutes the decisive moment; then the final words and the conclusion, which on the one hand refer back to the miracle and on the other refer to the reaction of those who were witnesses to the deed. This structure appears first at the literal level.

There is then the possibility of reading the same miraculous deed, respecting the inherent structure, within a liturgical perspective. What happens in Baptism, for example, corresponds to the structure of a miracle: thus in the first instance we see a person still captive to sin and evil; then there is immersion in water, which means conforming oneself to Christ in his death and burial. Finally there is emergence from the water, with all that follows for personal life, as well as its impact on all of those that are around that person.

The same gospel page can be also read at a more personal level. Each time that we find ourselves in sin we can find again the way to encounter Christ, calling on his Name through the sacrament of the Church or through the experience of prayer. Then once again the result will be a miracle made true and real in us, which will have its own repercussions around us. So we have three diverse ways of reading the same page of the gospel miracle, and all presuppose the literal meaning, which is given by the simplest structure comprising an introduction, a central part and a conclusion.

At other times the central moment, for example of a discourse of Jesus or the Apostles, can be grasped by considering that which constitutes the heart of the Church's confession of faith and the earliest apostolic *kerygma* or preaching of the death and resurrection of Jesus Christ. The whole page must be measured by this *kerygma*. From this derive some important consequences: the integrity of the discourse becomes apparent because it is attached to this fundamental point of teaching from which all depends. Think of the discourses of

Peter and of the Apostles in the Acts of the Apostles: there is always this central frame of reference, without which the story would miss its true foundation. In some discourses, then, we need to discover the core of the *kerygma* around which all the rest is constructed.

It may then be observed that some pages of the New Testament are constructed on the model of the journey of faith, as it is still lived today in the sacraments of Christian initiation. Think of the cure of the man born blind in John 9, or of Jesus' encounter with the Samaritan woman in John 4. There is a progression in the journey of faith of these two persons. Generally it is possible to highlight this progression by paying attention to the titles by which Jesus is called or described. Initially he might be called 'Jesus of Nazareth', then 'Master', then 'Son of David' and finally 'Messiah', or even 'Son of God' (cf. John 1.43–51). There is a progression in the awareness of Jesus in the mysterious reality of his life, comparable to progress in embracing the faith during the catechumenal journey. Very often this type of structure is encountered as a pattern for life 'in the way': it starts from a certain level and it progresses, advancing by subsequent steps, each identified with the titles of Christ.

On other occasions again we face pages that reflect the structure of baptismal immersion. They start from a very negative situation and then move towards a positive end. For example the structure of the story of the disciples walking to Emmaus (Luke 24.13–35): at the beginning there is a negative situation. Hope dwindles until it almost disappears in despair: 'We had hoped . . . but it all ended.' At the culmination of despair appears a gleam of light, however, and a kind of education begins: Jesus takes by the hand the two disciples and, starting with Moses then the prophets and finally the psalms, he indicates to them, text by text, everything regarding himself in Holy Scripture. When he finally has prepared them, he leads them to the eucharistic banquet, breaks the bread, and there is the moment of recognition. From this there flow consequences: the disciples, after encountering Jesus through the Scriptures, are born anew and assume the courage of witnesses: the two run back, full of joy, to Jerusalem to give the news to the other apostles. This is the essential structure, moving from the low point and ascending always higher until it arrives at the act of witnessing.

It is not difficult to discover all this: it is sufficient to read with attention, and to follow the characters in this story. These disciples of Emmaus can, in some way, be followed in their own psychological attitude: they have been witnesses of the events in Jerusalem, and these tragic events have disconcerted them to the point of reaching the deepest despair. It is there that Jesus catches them. This is not the only example in which Jesus catches a person when at the low point of desperation. The miracles of Jesus often presuppose this situation in human life.

For the most part the centre of a gospel page does not have to be thought of as a geometric centre; instead it is the point of equilibrium. Sometimes what comes after the centre is very little, but the centre has such a weight as to create equilibrium in the text, because what is expressed in it has worked a radical change in the situation. Sometimes a story is constructed on two great pillars where the centre is constituted by the axis, which is the crowning point of the arch that springs from the two pillars.

On other occasions a text may be like the Annunciation to Mary (Luke 1.26–38). This text is constructed in such a way that everything finds its central reference point in the final conclusion, just as the dynamic manifestation of a plant tends towards the explosion of the flower and of the final fruit:

'Everything is possible to God.' This is the point of arrival in the story and it is put at the end. The structure then is more like a flower: there are the roots, there is the plant that grows, and then there is the final flowering. In this case it means nothing other than the conformity of the flesh of Mary to the Word and of the Word to the flesh, causing Mary to be the first to experience a transformation or transfiguration that is in some way a prophetic anticipation of the resurrection of the Lord. The 'resurrected' Mary then brings the announcement of Christ to Elizabeth.

According to Shouraki, a great contemporary Jewish theologian, commenting on the variety of literal structures in the biblical text, the pages of the Old Testament can sometimes be constructed on structures redolent of all manner of geometrical figures, flat ones as well as the three dimensional ones that we recognize. This may also be valid for the New Testament texts. The ancients had a mastery of text construction that is inconceivable for us.

The reverse of a flower-like structure, which needs to find its centre at the end, when the flower gives the fruit, is a structure with a pregnant beginning or principal affirmation: essentially the root is at the beginning and the rest is consequential. Such is the case of the 'Our Father' (Luke 11.2–4; Matthew 6.9–13), where everything hangs on the initial invocation. It is the case, according to some exegetes and some fathers, for example St Gregory of Nyssa, that the proclamation of the Beatitudes (Luke 6.20–26), has a similar pregnant beginning in its first affirmation: 'Blessed are the poor', or 'Blessed are the poor in spirit'. The body of all that follows cannot do without this central affirmation at the beginning, which gives colour to all the rest.

Familiarity with the Scriptures by steady reading

The structures of a biblical page are most diverse. It is clear that many times the acuteness of scholars is needed to highlight them; but often a careful reading, done with the help of a simple *sensus fidei*, a sense of faith and spiritual intuition, allows us to reach horizons apparently precluded for ever to those not initiated. All of this presupposes, naturally, a certain familiarity with the structures in the biblical text, and habitual participation in the liturgical and sacramental journey of the Church. Familiarity with Scripture is needed, then, that is close to the spirit of *Lectio Divina*. This is acquired only by reading the entire Bible in an extensive way. To do this thoroughly would require much time, simply reading and re-reading the text in every spare minute without more formal study. Only thus is familiarity with the Scriptures acquired.

First Origen, and then Jerome, utilized a method for themselves and their disciples intended to eliminate from their memory all that did not belong to the history of salvation. Obviously we can do this only if we are convinced that this is the most important thing, otherwise we would never find the time. We are too often committed to just causes, however, that do not allow us to find even two or three minutes for the Scriptures. This regular reading is important however; it is like preparing the soil in which *Lectio Divina* may be born. It is necessary however to be aware that neither regular reading of Scripture nor being up to date exegetically are to be identified with *Lectio Divina* itself: for this means a loving and direct encounter with the Word of God.

Close to this stands participation in the liturgical prayer of the Church, which is *Lectio Divina* done in a social context, according to the style of a specific Church community and its teaching. Origen used to say: 'As we have learned in the

Church, you should attempt afterwards in your life, in order to tap the fountain of your spirit.' This means that liturgical celebration is a paradigm for *Lectio Divina*. We must, in other words, search in order to enter into profound knowledge of the literal text, letting ourselves be educated by the liturgy of the Church, which teaches us to penetrate the hidden sense of the Holy Scriptures.

After analysis of the words and secondary phrases that have been identified as the most important parts of a single passage their sense must then be searched for. But there remains still much secondary material, in that same passage, which cannot and must not be simply eliminated. We have seen that after structural analysis, we can gradually arrive at the radical analysis that needs to be done based on the central verb governing the principal proposition. But what about all the other phrases and terms? Once we have adequately clarified the central term, all the rest will start to assume their position and the reason for their presence, and should not be considered as secondary. The fathers have taught us that not only can nothing be added to or taken away from Scripture; but that each small particular of the pages and of the words of Holy Scripture contains a wealth of infinite meanings.

Let us think, for example, of certain incidental observations by an author: for example that it was the sixth hour, that it was night, that it was during the first days of unleavened bread, that it was close to the Passover of the Jews. These are all incidental affirmations, apparently almost superfluous to the frame in which Jesus pronounces his most considered discourses. So for example in Matthew when it says: 'when he saw the crowds he went up a mountain. There he sat down, and when his disciples had gathered round him he began to address them' (Matthew 5.1–2). It would have been enough for him to say: 'he went up the mountain and proclaimed' or 'he went up the mountain and started to proclaim'. But Matthew cares about details: through them we understand that we are encountering a master with authority, who from the desk of his writing transmits a message which is not any ordinary message, but contains the very Word of God.

These observations and many others like them are not only what we would call the frame of the picture, but also determine its colour and necessary perspective, by which we may look at a precise painting in order to understand its hidden secret and its message. Without this colour, it would only be with great difficulty that we would be able to catch the profound sense of a page of the gospel. Very often the bond of love that establishes itself between the reader and a particular page of the Bible is due really to the wholeness of those little phrases that constitute precious touches of light and warmth, without which the painting itself would have appeared austere or cold and insignificant. There are then certain contexts, certain roots and associations that come out of a page of Scripture and that intrigue us in a particular way, just because of these incidental details that we may initially have excluded for an instant.

4

Following Jesus in the gospel

Lectio Divina *on Matthew 8.18–22*

This is the moment to open the Bible. We do so at the Gospel of Matthew 8.18–22, set for reading within the eucharistic liturgy. Independently from the prompting of the liturgy, we could have chosen any one of the Gospels and practised on some perhaps more attractive passages. I believe though that it is fruitful to proceed with the daily liturgical passages, even when at first they can seem arid. This sheds much more light upon that profound comprehension of the Scriptures that is the gift of the Spirit. Given that the whole Church prays every day to understand the sense of the portion proposed for the liturgy, we also must put ourselves in communion with her prayer, and the Lord will not leave us unsatisfied. Welcoming our part in the humble and poor journey of the Church, we also will engage in an act of trust towards the Holy Spirit.

Careful reading of the text

The first step, opening the book of the Scripture, is to read the chosen text. Let us now do so now: 'At the sight of the crowd surrounding him Jesus gave word to cross to the other side of the lake. A scribe came up and said to him, "Teacher, I will follow you wherever you go." Jesus replied, "Foxes have their holes and birds their roosts; but the Son of Man has nowhere to lay his head." Another man, one of his disciples said to him, "Lord, let me go and bury my father first." Jesus replied, "Follow me, and leave the dead to bury their dead."'

It would not be enough to read this only once to be able to claim to have read it with attention: we need to read the passage two or three times, understanding point by point what the page is saying. There are techniques for careful reading similar to memorization: the ancient monks often used these. The Pachomian monks, for example, established in their rules that nobody could be welcomed as a postulant, until they could prove that they knew by memory at least the book of Psalms. A postulant otherwise stayed outside the monastery, sleeping in the open air, all the time necessary to memorize the Psalter. Anyone who wanted to enter into the monastery to pursue the journey towards God had to demonstrate how to show attention to the Word of God.

Even today memorization can be useful. With it the temptation of sleep can be conquered, which assaults us not only in our corporate engagement with *Lectio Divina* in church, but also in prayer by ourselves in the privacy of our bedroom, study or cell. Another technique is that of translation from the original text, or perhaps translation from another known language. This can concentrate the attention. Each person will choose the technique that corresponds to his or her own need and to his or her own possibilities. Different translations also can be considered in the same language, and through recognition of their diversity attention is maintained. When you are aware that you are reading without attention, however, start again from the beginning. It does not help at all to read without attention. Read maybe a little, but with awareness.

The structure of the text

Let us move to the next step: to discern the structure of the text, in other words its mode of construction. In each construction first the base or the foundations are laid, then the walls are raised, finally the closing of the roof is accomplished. Each page of the Scripture is a similar construction. But not all types of constructions are the same. It is one thing to construct a Coliseum, another to construct a basilica like St Peter's. Diverse though they are, they both have their own logic or plan of construction. Structural plans are as varied as constructions. This is equally true of each page of the Old and New Testaments. There are structures that answer more or less to the same principles; but it is always necessary to discover the foundation from which the author has started and then climb up the walls with him.

Let us return to the five verses of our text for today: in them there are two types of foundation, two sayings of Jesus, two specimens of the oral tradition. It is easy enough to identify them. The first is in verse 20: Jesus answered: 'Foxes have their holes and the birds their roosts; but the Son of Man has nowhere to lay his head.' This is the first part of the text. The second saying and second foundation that is introduced is: 'Follow me, and leave the dead to bury their dead.'

If Jesus' sayings are the foundation of the text, the other elements must be examined in order to have a better comprehension of them, so that they might impress themselves on the heart of the listener. Let us see by careful reading which are the added elements: 'At the sight of the crowd surrounding him Jesus gave word to cross to the other side of the lake. A scribe came up and said to him, "Teacher, I will follow you wherever you go."' Jesus' answer is intended to clarify the implications arising from the question of the scribe, who did not realize the commitment that he would have to make by presenting his question to the Lord. Perhaps this deeper reflection on the text was the meditation of the scribe Matthew, who constructed it all: it is as if Matthew were to say: 'But do you know where this teacher intends to go?' The saying of Jesus highlights the consequences of the willingness of the scribe. But it will be necessary to go deeper. Let us examine meanwhile the preceding phrase: 'At the sight of the crowd surrounding him Jesus gave word to cross to the other side of the lake.'

What was the need to create this kind of introduction? Was it not already enough to present the scribe? If the author of the Gospel has retained this detail as necessary, to be able to frame better the answer of Jesus, then there must be a reason for this introduction. Let us remember that we are in a context immediately following the Sermon on the Mount. Jesus reveals himself with deeds, with miraculous signs. Think about the leper being cured, about the Roman centurion, about the mother-in-law of Peter. Let us remember all the healing of the sick, of the possessed, that allows the evangelist to conclude: 'He took our illnesses from us and carried away our diseases' (Matthew 8.17, quoting Isaiah 53.5).

Then we become aware of being confronted by the Suffering Servant of second Isaiah, and also by the passion of Jesus, who has burdened himself with all that is negative in humanity, and who has taken on himself the sins of the world and borne them away. The fruit is the conquest of the great multitude, in whose presence Jesus now orders crossing to the other shore. The command to cross to the other shore is then very important. It can be seen perhaps as comparable to the crossing of the Red Sea, but most of all that of the River Jordan: Jesus will lead them into the Promised Land. The question of the scribe then becomes a question set within the Promised Land; and the sense of the text receives enlightenment, which illuminates a great range of practical consequences.

Deepening the sense of the text by meditation

We have seen that the first step of *Lectio Divina* consists in the search for the literal sense. However we know that, at least in the monastic tradition, the text, respected in its literal sense, has an infinite range of meaning: and it is not hyperbole to say an infinite range. The ancient fathers arrive at this affirmation, starting from their own concept of God: being about and by containing the Word of God, Scripture has in some way the attributes of God. Because God by definition is without limits, the Word that comes from the abyss, which is the mystery of God, must be infinite. This is why nobody can pretend to exhaust the sense of a text of Scripture: it always remains open, and each person can and must tap it in the measure by which he or she is capable. The capacity to tap in this way is at the root of the capacity for meditation, which is the second step.

The attitude of Mary – an example of meditation

When speaking of meditation in the spirit of Scripture, the word refers us to the attitude of Mary receiving the words of the angel (Luke 1.26–38), encountering the words of Simeon (Luke 2.22–35), or reflecting on the very words of Jesus. This means that the Christian who wants to enter a deeper attitude of meditation can find no better point of reference than the attitude of Mary. Luke asserts that Mary did not understand all that was said to her at the time; however she kept the words in her heart and she pondered them. Her quiet authority, born of long meditation, lies behind the text we now have in the Gospel.

The term 'to ponder' comes from the Greek word *symbolizing*, which is a composite of the preposition *sin*, 'with', and the verb *baleen*, 'to throw'. One has almost the impression that the heart of Mary, the interior life of Mary, becomes in the vision that Luke gives, a kind of furnace in which these words are thrown around, amalgamating in a reciprocal way, almost dissolving and then in some way clarifying each other. An image habitually used by the Church fathers is one of rocks dragged by a river: when they arrive at the sea, they are so burnished as to become surprisingly brilliant carriers of light or mirrors with which one can contemplate. So in Mary the words engage each other: they burnish themselves and become translucent, even transparent, each one the image of the other. This is the meaning of meditation in pursuit of *Lectio Divina*: we do not intend anything other than this.

The phases of meditation

Meditation according to most ancient monastic tradition comprises three movements, that result, according to the guidance of the fathers, from the fusing of two images drawn from the book of Proverbs: that of the ant (Proverbs 6.6–11) and that of the bee (placed in the tradition of the Septuagint immediately after that of the ant, although it is not in the Vulgate tradition, that derives directly from the Hebrew text; it is possible to find it in a note in the Jerusalem Bible).

The phase of gathering

What does consideration of the ant in the book of Proverbs indicate? It is a call to stay awake: awake before the Word of God. All distraction is eliminated for that is nothing other than the fruit of our torpor. It is vital to be awake to provide for oneself and to put laziness aside. The fathers define the attitude of the ant by the Greek verb 'to gather' or 'to bring together', from which comes the word *syntaxes* that means 'gathering'. This gathering is in fact the first phase of meditation. At this point there is no concern as yet about consuming the food: that also will have to happen, but the first thing is to gather it, wherever it may be found. How can we begin to search for this food? The fathers teach about this too.

We have seen that the search for the literal sense concludes with grinding the key word, which is pivotal to the whole construction. The hammering of such a word produces, according to the fathers, some insights that glance upon other passages of Holy Scripture, that are then seen as a unity. While we pound words, using the techniques described, a particular word enlightens us immediately by a moment of remembrance, recalling to us another passage, another aspect of Scripture. There, where our memory stops, we must gather the fruit. This is why we must not simply utilize the gathering done by others: we would risk too cold an encounter. What is important is that we pound the actual word of the page, of a particular phrase, identifying the word that we have discerned to be the pivot of the whole passage. The gathering must be personal: this is a very important principle.

Obviously someone who has more familiarity with the Scriptures may gather a broader portion. But someone who has less familiarity should not be discouraged or envy those who gather more; he or she must be happy with that which they can gather. Here the ancient biblical tradition comes to our help: the manna in the desert had to be gathered according to the size of the family and according to their capacity to consume it, because gathering more led to its decay (Exodus 16). So each person must accept starting from his or her own maturity and creative capacity: in this way spiritual birth can occur.

According to an ancient tradition, Abraham, who was wise, wanting a son, expected a son by the promise of God born of spiritual intuition; but the son never appeared. Then Sarah, his wife, wise as well, said to Abraham: 'It does not help that you delude yourself about being able to have immediately the fulfilment of such a spiritual intuition: content yourself to generate children in this physical stage of your life, because you are not able to generate any other children.' Abraham obeyed Sarah and so Ishmael was born, the son of human wisdom. Only when Abraham became mature to the point of being no longer a great scientist, according to this ancient story, lost in numbering the stars, did he become completely open to the promise of the Lord. Then the moment occurred for the birth of the son of his spiritual intuition, Isaac, the son of joy and cheerfulness, a moment that comes to a person as the fruit of total abandonment to the hands of God. Much humility and much discretion is needed in gathering spiritual fruit: in the words of the psalmist: 'Lord, my heart is not proud, nor are my eyes haughty' (Psalm 131.1). We do not feel ready for this: for if we are at this beginning point, we must accept starting out from here, while obviously constantly reaching towards the highest, but accepting ourselves with all our limitations.

The word of Scripture, then, is first pounded; and where the sparks of this hammering settle, there we go and gather fruit according to our capacity for nourishment. This is to act like the ant. To be able to do this we have to observe the habits of the sages and become wise. The wise person is the one that does not abandon himself or herself to slumber but shakes from sleep. The time of inertia is finished, says the *Rule of Saint Benedict*: from the moment that you have had the intuition of the wealth hidden in the Word of God, go, sell all that you have, buy the land where the treasure is buried; because there, where your treasure is, will be your heart also (Matthew 6.21).

The phase of rumination or reflection

The second phase of meditation is what the ancients called thorough consideration; in Greek the word has its root in storing honey. Sometimes it is also called 'rumination' from the Latin word, but it means the same thing. When all the nutrient has been gathered in, the moment of enclosure in the cell of the heart comes, just as the bee does, there to cherish all that has been gathered.

According to the sayings of the fathers, the bee spoken of in the book of Proverbs (in the Septuagint) is the Church that honours wisdom, as Jesus affirms in the Gospel: 'God's wisdom is proved right by all who are her children' (Luke 7.35). Now wisdom in the tradition of the fathers is nothing other than the Word of God. It is about honouring the Scriptures, in other words surrounding them with all the warmth that allows the word to root well in our hearts, to blossom, to become a plant and to bring forth fruit. The fathers had a profound trust in the Word of God. Jesus himself affirmed that the most important thing is to sow the Word in soil ready to welcome it. Once the word has been sown, the farmer can go to sleep or dedicate himself to all the daily chores of his work. The word, like the seed, roots, blossoms, of its own accord, and at the moment of maturation produces fruit for the plucking. This is a sacramental vision of the Word of God, of something that produces fruit of its own, because it is the Lord who acts within us. But Jesus adds that it is vital to pay attention to the Word, to surround it with affection and attention, so that it will not be stolen from us.

In this second phase of the meditation there is also a reciprocal penetration happening far beyond our knowledge. For this the fathers often suggest reading the text that will be the object of *Lectio Divina* the preceding evening, because, even if we sleep, the Word of God in some way works within us and we find it already being ground as it were the next morning. We must then have greater trust in the capacity that the Word has to amalgamate itself with similar words by which it encounters us on its own terms.

The phase of encounter

Encounter characterizes the third phase of meditation. We have seen that the second phase of rumination requires from us simply care to guarantee the climate, the attention, the warmth, and the precaution that nobody steals from us this precious word. All the rest the Word does by itself. Through the third phase, however, is born a different attitude that the fathers called 'discernment'. The word in Greek speaks of *krisis* or judgement made with consent; it is about discernment that is a reciprocal clarification of the words that we have gathered within our own selves so that we keep custody of them and observe them.

Someone that becomes ever more aware of the clarity that emerges from this encounter, feels an inner confrontation or judgement. While the words clarify each other, something happens that may permeate us who are the recipients of these words. When a furnace is heated, it is not only the metal contained inside that becomes incandescent, the very walls receive the heat and it transforms them. Much more happens in us when, having gathered the words, we have given them the space in which they can confront us on their own terms and shed freely their brightness. During this encounter light shines forth; and if there is something that does not permit that light to permeate the whole, there comes a moment of judgement. It is the judgement that is born from the Word that convicts us. It is not something that comes from us. It is a brightness that shines forth from the Word, that Word that we have hammered, that word, for the explanation of which and for its brightness we have called for help using all the texts that we have found. It is a bright sword that transfixes us in our whole person (Hebrews 4.12–13).

It could be only an instant, just like a clap of thunder or flash of lightning that, in a moment of our life, brightens our whole person; or it could be a more persistent and stable light. In each case, from that moment on, one is not able to remain complacent; it is not possible to remain calm. That Word has become in us a devouring fire. It is at this point, and only at this point, that meditation will be able to transform itself into *oratio* – the prayer: 'Lord, save us for we perish!'

5

Lectio Divina and spiritual conflict

Matthew 8.23–27 – reading the text

Jesus then got into the boat, and his disciples followed. All at once a great storm arose on the lake, till the waves were breaking right over the boat; but he went on sleeping. So they came and woke him, saying: 'Save us, Lord; we are sinking!' 'Why are you such cowards?' he said. 'How little faith you have!' With that he got up and rebuked the wind and the sea, and there was a dead calm. The men were astonished at what had happened, and exclaimed: 'What sort of man is this? Even the wind and the sea obey him.'

Analysis of the structure

A particular detail reveals itself in the Greek text. At the beginning it speaks to us of 'his disciples', in the last verse, there is the expression 'the men' in general. It is a notable difference because it obliges us to distinguish between what appears to the disciples and what appears in other men's reactions.

In verses 23–26 there are two very precise correspondences. In verse 24 it says in the original text: 'and behold a violent tempest was unleashed'. The Greek literally says: 'and behold a great *seismos* occurred in the sea'. The word *seismos* can mean either a hurricane or an earthquake, and it is the same expression that Matthew uses when he recounts the resurrection of Jesus. This association opens another horizon that deepens the contrast when calm descends after the storm, for a great shaking is balanced by a great calm. We must discover where the transition from the great upheaval to the great serenity occurs. The heart of the passage has to be searched for between these two extremes.

In the first part we have the consequences of the great upheaval of the sea: the boat is almost submerged, overwhelmed and engulfed by the waves. The Greek word used can also mean 'hidden' or 'engulfed' and the word *apokalypto,* 'to reveal', is its opposite. The sea and the waves that threaten to submerge the boat are in some sense a manifestation of evil. This evil threatens to engulf the whole boat, to the point of submerging it. But here the observation occurs: 'Jesus was asleep.' It is another neat *chiaroscuro*: on the one hand the sea in its tempest engulfs everything, and on the other Jesus is inside the boat with the others, but asleep. Mark adds that he was asleep on a pillow, underlining the placidity of his sleep.

For Jesus the sea and the upheaval of its waves is simply a comfortable bed, a cradle of rest. A bright spark of association points to the sign of Jonah that is being fulfilled (Matthew 12.38–40). Obviously we are facing an Easter situation. There are pointers calling for meditation here: Jesus appears completely submerged by the power of evil; he is buried in some way in the darkness. And not only him, but also everyone in the boat is in the same situation. The others are being submerged with him and in their desperation they cannot forbear shouting out: 'Save us, Lord, we are lost!'

They must shake Jesus, to wake him up. In the parallel text of Luke the Greek verb *diegheiran* is used, while here we have *eigheran*, which is the technical term for wakefulness. The preposition *dià* in St Luke indicates that they were not satisfied to wake him up by calling but by shaking him, taking him by the arm or even moving his head: 'Wake up! Wake up! We are going to die!' Agitation and fear dominated them, as Jesus remarks: 'Why are you afraid?' They could not be otherwise: there is a hidden contrast between the attitude of Jesus who sleeps and the agitation of the disciples, who cannot cope with their desperation and so address themselves to him. They call him *Kyrie*, or 'Lord'. It is an indication that we are already in the context of the life of the Church. A further point for meditation: in Mark the word used is 'Master', and in Luke the word used is *Epistata*, which means 'chief' or 'supervisor', one that stands as head over the others: 'you are our chief, wake yourself up!'

The agitation of the disciples makes them aware of their own sense of littleness, of their impotence in the face of disaster and evil. It induces insistent prayer that the Lord would wake up and change the whole situation. Now the word *Kyrie*, or perhaps the whole invocation: 'Lord save us!' seems to be the heart of the text, along with the phrase: 'We perish!' This invocation is the turning point because in response Jesus awakes and arises and his efficacious word restores peace, the calming of the sea and the joy of the apostles. Thus the invocation of verse 25: 'Lord, save us! We perish!' assumes the central point in the text: it is a great note of hope for their small community. When any Christian community finds itself in a similar situation, it knows what it must do: it must grasp hold of this invocation.

The text continues: '"Why are you such cowards?" he said, "How little faith you have!" With that he got up and rebuked the wind and the sea, and there was a dead calm.' We have now arrived at that contrasting point to which we referred at the start. To conclude then, this text presents a dramatic situation, which is an experience similar to that of prayer. Such is the teaching that seems to result from the literal reading of the text: each dramatic situation is its own appropriate moment for invocation, and the Lord will command the winds and the sea and guarantee the serenity which we need.

This happened inside the boat, and it happens inside the Church community; and as it is told, it becomes a proclamation of missionary witness. The men see something real and are overtaken by great awe. This awe is the miracle that awakens in man the attitude of amazement and wonder, what the Old Testament calls 'the fear of the Lord'. They gave themselves up for lost, but it was enough that they said: 'Lord, save us – we are perishing!' for everything to return to peace.

Their missionary testimony is this: the other men were filled with wonder, saying: 'But who is this person whom even the wind and the sea obey?' They do not speak of the boat, but of Jesus: the boat by then was already virtually lost, but he, being called, has been able to create a situation that is radically renewed. The question contains already the answer, because the reference is in Genesis 1, to the Word that creates in the very moment that it is pronounced; and also to the one who led the chosen people into the Promised Land, Joshua, who commanded the sun in order to guarantee victory to the people of God (Joshua 10.12–14; cf. also Psalm 77.16–20).

6

The birth of prayer

Oratio – prayer from within

The light that reveals itself in the encounter that is prayer brightens the situation in which we find ourselves, and it kindles the experience of *oratio*: not in the sense that all our experience so far in our life was not in some way prayer; but rather in the sense of an awareness of the incomprehensible or ineffable utterance of the Spirit that emerges from within, that breaks out into words in a way not possible before.

The prayer of compunction

This *oratio*, this prayer, is the fruit of our encounter with the Word of God. It assumes diverse forms, according to the necessity that each one of us perceives within. The fathers distinguished various types of *oratio*.

The first is the *oratio compunctionis*, which is like a trans-fixing of the heart, a sense of self-abandonment, even of apparent annihilation. Let us think of Isaiah in the temple: he feels the impurity of his lips (Isaiah 6.5) and throws himself face down, asking with all his heart for purification. It is also the attitude of the hearers of St Peter on the day of Pentecost. They faced a call so strong that they felt their hearts transfixed

(Acts 2.37), unable to avoid confessing their own need of radical conversion. The Word of God, as in this case, reaches into us like a sword of light, which cuts us from head to toe and renders us naked (Hebrews 4.12). The consequences are tears, the sense of our own nothingness, of our whole situation of sin; and then the spontaneous commitment to initiate the journey of radical conversion. There are people that remain entire months and years in this journey nurtured by their tears. St Romuald even exhorted his disciples not to cry too much lest they dissolved in tears of compunction before the Word of God. This is the first manifestation of *Lectio Divina* becoming prayer and transforming our life. *Oratio compunctionis* is essentially personal, because each person comes with their own life, with its betrayals and particular situations of sin. It can express itself even in cries of pain; but very often it is a secret transfixing that we experience inwardly, that we cannot and must not reveal to others.

Oratio petitionis – intercession

Progressing in our encounter with the Word of God, the sword of light can make us aware of our binding covenant with the Lord, despite our many failures and the poverty that accompanies too often our range of choices, which we now want to pursue with firmer commitment. In this case prayer becomes easily *oratio petitionis*, or intercession. We must not discourage ourselves, for it is as if Jesus says: 'Do not be destructive to your own selves; do not say: "I cannot change", or "it is useless".' Instead Jesus says: 'Until now you have asked nothing in my name. . . . So I say to you, ask, and you will receive; seek, and you will find; knock, and the door will be opened to you. For everyone who asks receives, those who seek find, and to those who knock, the door will be opened' (Luke 11.9–10).

The important thing is to ask in the name of Jesus for the gift of the Spirit anew, and certainly the answer will come. This also is the fruit of our encounter with the Word of God. And the more we nourish ourselves with the Word, the more we are aware of not being able to do so without asking: because the Word becomes incarnate within us, it compels us from within. We can do everything to try to exclude it from our lives, but it reasserts itself again and anew.

So even when we have to admit to not being sufficiently faithful, when we have to admit to our daily sinfulness, let us seek to preserve at least some contact with the Word of God. Then, sooner or later, this Word will oblige us to change our life. Even if what remains now is only our covenant of commitment to *Lectio Divina*, around it will be constructed all our lives: because it is Christ himself who is at the door knocking (Revelation 3.20). If we do not send him away, but allow him to knock, sooner or later the door of our heart will open.

Eucharistic *oratio*

It may be that the sword of divine light has entered within us and has confronted us with a personal or social story in the Bible, that in light of the Word, we recognize with amazement to be a story of salvation. All the moments of our lives, even the moments of unfaithfulness, all the encounters with other persons, however ambiguous they may have been, seen in reality in the light of the Word, become moments of salvation, what St Irenaeus calls 'constant economies of God in favour of man'. The word 'economy' in this sense means 'saving' because of the providential attitude of God towards the circumstances of our personal existence.

In the light of the Word all situations, even the most fallible, acquire a saving value: it is enough to think of the history of Israel. Even the moment in which Israel had completely lost orientation becomes in the hands of God an occasion of new revelation, broader, greater, more encompassing of his attention. Even the Exodus is not the final word, for the sin of God's people in the desert never has the last word: the last word belongs always to the Lord. The last word is in fact the victory over sin: for the Lord delivers us when we are not capable of delivering ourselves.

Awareness of this action of the Lord transforms prayer into *eucharistic oratio*, that is into a prayer of thanksgiving; because with amazement we see that our lives have been directed by someone who has accompanied us with providential loving, with the foresight of a mother. Where we have fallen, he has transformed our weaknesses into experiences of maturation. We have become stronger, more mature, and on account of this we are perhaps more aware of the gift we may now offer to the Lord.

Oratio laudativa – the prayer of praise

There is, finally, an attitude that touches on the ecstatic characteristic of childhood, that expresses itself when the Word of God fills us simply with joy and we do not know what to say beyond that it is beautiful, and we do not know either how to declare how beautiful it is. It is a taste that certainly we have all experienced in our childhood; but it is also a taste of the Word of God that we taste anew, when we find ourselves in particular moments of thankfulness, of spontaneity, of creativity, tasting what is beautiful and good. It is an experience that generally is not readily spoken of. It is the moment in which prayer is only *oratio laudativa*: a singing of praise, that is thanksgiving, request, compunction: all is in simple praise, a praise that accompanies us wherever we go, wherever we have a perception of being in the light of the Lord.

When *Lectio Divina* matures into prayer, it takes diverse roads. It cannot necessarily be said that they are sequential moments: they can be roads that intersect. Some time, for a long time, we may live only in one of the manifestations of prayer and we must simply once again accept ourselves as such with all our limitations, on the step on which, notwithstanding everything, we find ourselves, saying: 'Lord, my heart is not proud, nor are my eyes haughty' (Psalm 131.1).

7

Encounter with Christ

Lectio Divina *on Matthew 8.28–34*

Careful reading must be practised constantly and with patience. Sometimes texts are particularly difficult, like this passage about the exorcism of Legion that occupies in the whole New Testament a position that is somewhat solitary. It would be necessary to dig into the meaning of the pigs in Jewish cultural history, from the prehistoric times until today, to understand part of it. However there is the strange coincidence of the fight between Jesus and the possessed man (or according to Matthew the *two* possessed men) and the flight of the demon (or the legion of demons, according to Mark) into the herd of pigs: Mark indicates that the number afflicted was two thousand.

In comparison with the other Synoptic Gospels, it may be noted that the parallel texts of Mark and Luke are more extended and, I would say, also more complete, leading to an ending that is different from that of Matthew. Each evangelist is a witness to Jesus with his own personality and therefore with his own particular eyes. He has to be respected in his individuality. We could see here the origins of the diversity of Christian theology even when relating to a unique point of reference. The gospel is fourfold and – according to the fathers – its completeness is given by the wholeness of the number four. Naturally this fourfold gospel is binding for us. We cannot pretend to assume, with regard to the evident structure of the material, the same liberty that the four evangelists had. What they have transmitted to us is part of what we define as the deposit of revelation. However a certain theological pluralism can be traced back to the Gospels in their fourfold aspect.

Literal sense and structure

First of all let us try to point out, at least broadly, the literal meaning of this passage in order to enlarge our meditation. Let us read the text.

> When Jesus reached the country of the Gadarenes on the other side, two men came to meet him from among the tombs; they were possessed by demons, and were so violent that no one dared pass that way. 'Son of God,' they shouted, 'what do you want with us? Have you come to torment us before our time?' In the distance a large herd of pigs was feeding; and the demons begged him: 'If you drive us out, send us into that herd of pigs.' 'Go!' he said. Then they came out and went into the pigs, and the whole herd rushed over the edge into the lake, and perished in the water. The men in charge of them took to their heels, and made for the town, where they told the whole story, and what had happened to the madmen. Then the whole town came out to meet Jesus; and when they saw him they begged him to leave their district.

Reading this passage with attention, we note that there are two points of reference that can help us in our comprehension.

On the one hand there is the encounter of Jesus with the two possessed men; on the other the way in which the entire city confronts Jesus. Both of these are introduced by the phrase 'And behold', indicating a reprise in verses 29 and 34. These two situations interpose between the collision between Jesus and the devil, or the demons, in the two possessed men (a legion according to Mark and Luke). The impact reverberates in the strange phenomenon of the demoniacal possession of the herd of pigs. Although the possession of the pigs is incidental, the most important thing being the encounter between Jesus and the possessed men, and then with the people of the city, it gives vivid colour to the passage.

Another observation is that in the rendering by Matthew, Jesus strangely says only the word: 'Go!' – nothing more. The process that transforms the situation of the two possessed men, like that of the demons that possess them, happens almost automatically by itself. The demons are the ones that decide where to go in the end – Jesus does not do other than their desire: 'You want to go? Go!' It is evil that judges itself and in so doing also condemns itself. Jesus is only a condescending witness to their will. It is not difficult here to realize that maybe we are confronted with a divine judgement that we tend to restrict to the last times. Also in this moment the same word is pronounced, 'Go! – Go to the place prepared for you.' Everyone in other words is self-judged, and has extrapolated the consequences of that judgement. It is not Jesus that condemns. In the Gospel of St John this is most clear: 'I did not come to judge anyone' (John 3.17). There is something like a spontaneous development here for 'Go!' is the only word of Jesus (cf. Matthew 25.46).

A further observation regards the presence of Jesus that by itself is enough to transform the equilibrium of the region. Until Jesus arrives, the demons are the owners of the place, to the point that nobody can pass along that road, because they were so violent. Their power of death, underlined by the fact that they lived among the tombs, in the kingdom of destruction and of slavery to Satan, had the upper hand. The simple presence of Jesus turns this upside down. The presence of Jesus transforms also the equilibrium of human economic interests. The destruction of the herd of the pigs would in reality have forced onto their knees the local population that probably lived on the profit derived from it: two thousand pigs for one village are indeed many. It was maybe their principal industry, but now destroyed, however impure it would have been in the eyes of the Jews.

One final observation about the protest that the two possessed men, or the demons inside them, raised in regard to Jesus: 'Son of God, what do you want with us?' In the English translation the expression 'Son of God', written in capital letters, seems almost a confession of faith. In reality, if it is a mode of address, it could simply imply that Jesus is one son of God among many. In the pagan context in which Jesus acts it is, in fact, an expression that is ambiguous enough: the great benefactors of humanity were considered 'sons of God'. Such is the version in Matthew; in the rendering of Mark and Luke Jesus is addressed as 'Son of the Most High God'.

What can we conclude from the simple careful reading of this text? Two consequences: the first is about the two possessed men that are freed; for them the presence of Jesus is calming. The other consequence is about the city of the Gadarenes, which is a witness to this liberation, but having entered into a compromise with the kingdom of darkness, the kingdom of death, its inhabitants consider this action a threat to its power and so refuse Jesus entry.

From the Gospel of St Matthew we do not know what happened to the two freed men who had been possessed. From the other Synoptic Gospels we learn that the freed man went into the city to announce the miracle that had happened to him at the command of Jesus. He thus became the principal oral witness of the event and a missionary to his own people.

Meditatio

Let us move now to meditation. A key word is certainly the word, 'Go!' pronounced by Jesus that leads us also to the ending of Matthew 25, the parable of the Sheep and the Goats. Close in spirit to this reference are a series of other affirmations by Jesus, contained above all in the Gospel of John, in which he speaks of judgement, a judgement that happens inside each of us: between a person who is in the darkness and prefers to remain in the darkness, and one who is in the light, and not afraid of the light. This is an automatic judgement and its own affirmation is like a shining sword that cuts us within. Let us seek to respond immediately to its impact.

A second line of thought that arises from the text pertains to the relationship between Jesus and Satan. Immediately we recall the situation in which Jesus had to fight, face to face, with the devil. For example in Matthew 4.1–11, Jesus is called to encounter the devil in the desert, where he had been brought by the Holy Spirit, immediately to be tempted by the words, 'If you are the Son of God . . .': note the presence already here of the expression 'Son of God' used by the tempter. It is the temptation of power: 'The devil took him to a very high mountain, and showed him all the kingdoms of the world in their glory. "All these", he said, "I will give you, if you will only fall down and do me homage."' Also in this passage appears the city, the Holy City, in Luke more explicitly Jerusalem.

We can then associate with the fight between Jesus and

Satan other prophetic phrases, still in Matthew 4, in which Jesus is described as the one that brings light into the kingdom of darkness.

'The land of Zebulun, the land of Naphtali, the road to the sea, the land beyond Jordan, Galilee of the Gentiles: the people that lived in darkness have seen a great light; light has dawned on those who lived in the land of death's dark shadow.'

Matthew 4.15–16

It is a pagan land, a land abandoned to the grazing of impure animals, a region of death, darkness, and impurity, which now sees the light of Christ arise. The beginning of the Gospel of Matthew is constructed on the basis of manifesting the light of Christ in the darkness.

There is then another series of texts in Matthew that present the victory of Jesus on behalf of the possessed and the sick. Possessed and sick are put next to one another in this Gospel because sickness in the mind of Matthew is nothing other than a consequence of the possession of humanity by Satan. It is a tradition that goes back to the interpretation of the book of Genesis according to which, through the sin of Adam, death has entered the world, and illnesses are the consequences of the victory of Satan over man.

We arrive now at some of the strongest gospel texts, in which Jesus faces directly the nature of his fight with the Satan: Matthew 12.22–35 and 43–45. Jesus is victorious over the power of Satan, but there are some who instead of rejoicing show envy and try to insinuate into the minds of the people the idea that Jesus is able to send away the demons because he is an ally of them. It is not enough then that Jesus is victorious over the demons to ensure that the people believe him. Like the

Gadarenes that asked Jesus to distance himself, perhaps because they did not want to lose their economic security in response to the fate of the impure animals, so here the critics of Jesus do everything to convey a different colouring to the victory of Jesus over the demons. Jesus responds in a very uncompromising manner and it is here that he says: 'Every sin and every slander can be forgiven except slander spoken against the Holy Spirit; that will not be forgiven' (Matthew 12.31). This sin, in other words, consists of deliberately repudiating the truth notwithstanding its realization. It is rather like the sin of the Gadarenes, but it is also the sin of many others who, seeing Jesus triumph over Satan, instead of rendering glory to God, use the very fact to put Jesus in a bad light.

Jesus is instead much more accommodating when he confronts the fruit of the envy of the enemy present inside the Christian community: Matthew 13.24–30, with the subsequent explanation in verses 36–43, speaks of the sower of the good seed and of his enemy who sows tares. But Jesus is not so drastic or implacable as when he is face to face with Satan or with the envy of those who resist the Spirit. Here Jesus is more like a father, who accepts the family as it is, despite the negative sowing carried out by the evil one. To the apostles and the disciples that want to eradicate the tares immediately, he commands to wait while they grow together with the corn, with all that this implies in the historic journey of the Church: not to seek a fundamentalist integrity, but to grow in proximity to the worldly situation of men and women. At the end of times the angels of the Shepherd will arrive to separate corn and tares, throwing these into the fire. It is not up to us to eradicate those we judge to be tares: we would risk eradicating also the good plants.

Let us refer also to the Old Testament in relation to the fight between Jesus and Satan: the fight between David and Goliath, seen by the fathers' typological interpretation of this story as an epitome of the history of the people of Israel. The fight is between this small insignificant people and these who inhabit the earth and have contaminated it, according to the biblical tradition, with their evil works. The people of Israel act like a purifying fire, also epitomized in the figure of Elijah. We arrive finally at the theme of the pure and the impure, certainly one of the more pregnant elements of the text. The distinction between impurity and purity is one of the most important criteria in the religious tradition of the Old Testament: what is impure must be eliminated and what is pure must be guaranteed. Reading the Pentateuch, notably Leviticus, it is evident how much insistence the tradition of Moses laid upon the importance of legal purity and especially of the sacral purity of the priests. For the Holy One is essentially pure and so whoever gets close to him must be pure also. From this arises not only the proscription of consuming anything impure, but also of not frequenting an environment that might contaminate them by its impurity.

The discourse of Jesus on this theme is therefore totally innovative, indeed revolutionary. He goes to the other shore, to the region of the impure. His sign is prophetic. In fact the demons ask him why he has gone there before the time: before which time? Probably before the time of the Church, which starts with the mission that Jesus commands at the end of Matthew 28, where he says: 'All authority has been given to me in heaven and earth. Go then and make disciples of all nations' (Matthew 28.18–19). This may be reflected in the other two Gospels, which portray the liberated man as a missionary to his own people and perhaps intimating that his story became the seed of a church in Gentile territory.

'Why did you come before the time?' The question may be

posed polemically inside the primitive Christian community to Peter but also to Paul. Peter is the first to break the barrier and the distinction between pure and impure: in chapter 10 of the Acts of the Apostles he has his famous vision of the table-cloth full of animals of each kind, and the injunction to take and eat and not to judge as impure any more what the Lord has cleansed, which should now be considered pure.

In the text of Matthew there is then an answer to a situation in the primitive Church, in which there was still conflict over the distinction between pure and impure. Peter realizes that the Lord no longer makes any distinction between persons but belongs to the person who is pure in heart. The community may also find in the example of Jesus in the region of the impure a reference point that would justify going among pagans without fear of contaminating themselves. Jesus, by going among the impure, has eliminated impurity and has made captive Satan and the impurity that gathers itself around him, throwing it into the depths of the sea. It is similar to much that will happen according to the Apocalypse at the end of times, when death will be overthrown and cast forever into the lake of fire.

In the problem of the primitive community and in its transcendence lies perhaps the central message of our text: 'Do not judge anymore impure that God forever has judged pure' (Acts 10.15).

This is also implied in the prophetic announcement of the universality of salvation: when Jesus said that he was not sent only to the house of Israel but to the lost sheep among the Gentiles, he gives prophetically a start to the demolition of the restricted borders of Israel. To see the full scope of this message it is necessary to look at the passage in Matthew 15.10–28, in which there is the discourse about what is pure and impure, and which concludes with the encounter and cure of the Canaanite child. This Gentile child is the representative of what is impure: first of all because she is a possessed female and then because she is pagan. Jesus confronted by the sincere insistence of the Canaanite mother changes his mind. He who came only for the lost sheep of the house of Israel, and who initially responded that it is not good to take the children's bread to give it to the dogs (because pagans were regarded by many Jews as dogs and pigs), when confronted by her insistence changes his outlook and answers: 'What faith you have! Let it be as you wish!' The story of the exorcism among the Gadarenes therefore opens to us horizons beyond borders. The message of Jesus is the proclamation of a potentially universal salvation.

What will be the prayer that will be born from this meditation? It may possibly be a prayer of thanksgiving to the Lord because he has offered us a horizon beyond the borders of our own experience, in which finally we find ourselves again. For notwithstanding the knowledge of our own impurity, we trust in the will of the Lord to take care of us. Obviously we cannot limit ourselves in prayer to our simple personal individuality or social existence. We are invited by this text to expand our hearts towards all human salvation. Certainly when Jesus arrives, among us and among the pagans, he arrives like a purifying fire, not leaving things as they are but as the liberator from impurity. There is then a responsibility kindled for those that encounter him, and for them will occur many occasions for prayer.

8

The flowering of new senses

Contemplation as a return to paradise

The fourth step of *Lectio Divina* is traditionally defined as one of contemplation. There is a persistent definition of contemplation that identifies the taste of an unspeakable experience, which grows in the heart of the person who makes of the Word of God the sole point of reference for their life. It represents a mode of access that implies some risks, however, entailing the enclosing of oneself so that through the road of *Lectio Divina*, meditation, and prayer, an experience of a 'return to paradise' occurs. This could be identified with a return to the warm maternal womb where all is given, all is lived in the most gracious way, and where everything can enclose itself within a certain insensibility for that which now lies outside. Certainly contemplation becomes like a 'return to paradise', taking into consideration the risk of living an experience limited to the 'closed garden' of the soul, with a fence that protects you, that allows you to plumb the depths of the Word of God and that however at the same time closes you to the outside world.

Not all the fathers have followed such a conception of contemplation, however. This description of contemplation by Guigo of Chartreux, is typical of the conception that we have described:

The eyes of the Lord are on the just and His ears are mindful of their prayers to the point where, not wanting even that the prayer be concluded, He intervenes in the very course of prayer, and rushes to enter into the soul that searches for Him with desire. He rushes to encounter her, drenched in the glory of celestial sweetness and scented with precious ointments that recreate the tired soul, sustaining in light one who is thirsty and nurturing that which is hungry. He makes her forget the things of the earth and He brings her alive, making her admiringly forgetful of herself, and scenting her renders her sober. It is similar to certain carnal acts, when the soul is won to such a degree by the concupiscence of the flesh as to lose all use of reason and the person becomes temporarily almost completely carnal; so but on the contrary, in this superior contemplation, all carnal dynamics are virtually transcended and absorbed by the soul, so that the flesh in no way contradicts the spirit, and the person becomes almost completely spiritual.

But O Lord, how will we know when you do this? And what is the sign of your coming? Are not tears and sighs perhaps messengers and witnesses of the advent of this contemplation and joy? If this is so, is this a new insinuation or intimate sign? . . . O blessed tears by which interior stains are washed away and the fire of sin extinguished! Blessed are you who so cry, because you will laugh. Recognize, my soul, in these tears the nearness of your heavenly Bridegroom. Embrace him for whom you struggle within yourself in desire. Scent yourself now in the torrent of His good pleasure; drink now from the fountain of milk and honey that is His consolation.

But why do we proffer in public these secret conversations? Why do we attempt to express them, using common words, feeling and tenderness that are unspeakable? Those who have not experienced such joy cannot understand; they would better understand it by reading about them in the book of spiritual experience, where may be found the true divine anointing that disciplines the soul.

> *Guigo was the ninth prior of La Grande Chartreuse in France, and died in 1193. He is the author of 'Scala claustralium' and 'Scala paradisi'*

This is a description of contemplation perceived as a return to the maternal womb, in which a person feels completely satisfied and in which all the rest is forgotten, because it has been transcended; because confronted by the experience of the Spirit, nothing that refers to the flesh serves any purpose at all. The risk, as we said, is that of forgetfulness of the world and of its history. However in contrast to this, other fathers have used the term contemplation in a different way.

Contemplation as the irruption of the divine into history

We need to remind ourselves of the etymology of the Latin term *contemplatio*, in order to realize its own resonance that normally escapes us, the term having become so usual in monastic and religious tradition. Contemplation is a term formed from two words: the preposition *cum*, meaning 'with', and the substantive word *templatio*, which has a reference to the noun, *templum*, meaning 'temple'. The word 'temple' recalls the symbol of a temple, that in itself refers to the horizons of the cosmos: for the temple is most of all that which we identify with the heavens. The temple is thus a cupola mirroring the celestial vault that circumscribes the space in which we live out our historic experience; but it is also something that hides the beyond, for the Latin word *coelum* comes from *celare* that means 'to hide'.

Seen and interpreted in this way, the temple symbolizes on the one hand the embrace of the whole world within the sign of a reality that is beyond us; and on the other hand it indicates the limit beyond which the invisible One dwells, He that is veiled by this limited horizon of ours. To live this contemplation means, in this case, living within the temple, inside the sacred space circumscribed by that contemporary place that is a location within the limit set; as the location also where the transcendent is intuited as being accessible beyond that limit, just as He who remains invisible welcomes the universe and embraces it. The contemplative person can then be perceived as someone who lives inside a space that assumes our concrete life, in order to open it to that eternal history that we Christians identify with the divine or Trinitarian life.

At this point we could add that the place of the highest contemplation has been revealed in the person of Jesus of Nazareth, born from Mary. For in him, in order to accomplish the incarnation of the Word of God, there has been the perfect conjunction between heaven and earth, between what is beyond the celestial veil and what is on this side and which we identify with the earth. From this we may conclude that the culmination of contemplation lies not in separating what is spiritual from what is material, but in the most perfect union possible between heaven and earth, between the divine and the human, the vertical dimension and the horizontal. The person who could achieve the synthesis of these two realities would in fact become authentically contemplative.

Remaining close to the spirit of *Lectio Divina*, we could add also another thing: that it is in our realizing the experience of contemplation, in meditation upon the Word of God, that in a specific text, letter or words, quite visible to the eyes of our flesh, we discover the living person of the Word of God and the presence of the Holy Spirit.

Synthesis between word and spirit: this is perhaps the essence of contemplation. Obviously this is not about a mental or intellectual vision, but of a vital reality. We have insisted much on obedience to the letter, to the discipline of not escaping its demand in order to remain within the spiritual indication that comes from the visibility of the letter; just as we would insist that if we had the person of Jesus as our object of thought, we should not depart from the visibility of his fleshly existence in history: because *cardo salutis caro*, the cardinal principle of our salvation is in the flesh of Christ. The cardinal point of our spiritual development lies in the letter, the written word that is quite visible to our eyes and equally audible to our ears. In the synthesis between the sacred and the mundane, between the letter and the Spirit, our vision expands necessarily to embrace all that constitutes visible reality and also that reality which surrounds human life in space and history.

In the contemplative journey we start with discovering what falls under our senses, learning from minerals, plants, animals; then from the events that express themselves in time, because everything is a manifestation of the Word of God. But then encounter with Holy Scripture becomes for us equally fertile, as in the encounter with the historic event of Jesus of Nazareth. In it we tap the fountainhead of that light, which permits us to discover its presence also in those writers of far distant times, which we did not first understand well, but who received the presence of the Word. Frequenting this fountain and getting closer to it, we come to recognize with simplicity that this fountain has already spoken through history and continues to speak still in history to us today.

In reality it is as if we fulfil, through *Lectio Divina*, training in the same search for the Word of God in the written words of the Bible that is repeated continually throughout history, in the midst of all the progress of our humanity. In our case it fills us also with awe by the same transition: from the letter to the Spirit, from the words to the Word. Each single personal and social event reveals itself as threads interwoven within the text of history. The ancient fathers saw in all history a logical connection, which they simply identified with the Logos or Word of God, hidden or sown in the words of history, that can only be recognized by beginning with Jesus of Nazareth, the Son of God.

At this point we could conclude that the contemplative person is one in whom has been achieved a synthesis between what is divine and what is human, because he or she has been completely caught by the Word of God and therefore is able by a certain affinity to perceive the infinitesimal smallest presence of the Word of God that is in each reality in the cosmos and in history.

The contemplative has been, is, and forever now will be, not a person divorced from history, but one who has the eyes of the heart so acute as to be able to see the presence of the Word of God, even where others would see only the presence of evil and sin. For this reason the contemplative is fundamentally an optimist, one who reveals or conveys the beautiful and the new, being like Isaac, a child of laughter and of gratuitous spiritual intuition. A person that is wholehearted, that opens the eyes of others, that never loses courage, because he or she knows for sure that even in the most dramatic of events, even in the most sinful situation, there is always that spark of the divine Logos, of the Word of God, who died and who was resurrected. The contemplative person knows, in fact, that always, and from each angle, even in the most obscure things of the earth, each existence calls insistently to its Lord.

Contemplation as the vision of Christ
crucified and risen

By the definition of contemplation, strictly derived from the etymology of the Latin term *contemplatio*, we have seen how far the contemplative person becomes close to history and is optimistic in confronting human history, and so becomes someone who can guide others by the hand towards the One who is the fulfilment of their own history.

But there is another way to consider contemplation, which starts from the etymology of the words used in Greek to indicate it: *theoria*. In English the word 'theory' indicates an abstract principle in opposition to pragmatism. The Greek term however is the synthesis of two very interesting terms: *thea* and *orao*. *Thea* means 'vision', but a vision in the panoramic sense of the word. *Orao* on the other hand means simply 'to see'. When it is said 'to see a vision', or 'to see in a vision', it means that how we look is not superficial, but rather reinforced by our intention: 'I look and see', or perhaps 'I observe and see': it is like entering in to what one observes. There is only one reference point for the use of the Greek word *theoria* in the Christian tradition however: the crucified Christ. Luke uses, for the only time in the entire New Testament, the word *theoria* uniquely to indicate the vision of Christ crucified on the Calvary (Luke 23.48).

For the ancient fathers this means that a person who has the gift of the *theoria*, of contemplation, is always one who stands before the mystery of Christ crucified, as the Word that reveals the meaning of all history. In this case the contemplative becomes the person that looks at all the wrinkles of human history and of the world by starting from the vision of the crucified Christ, a vision that becomes inherently an announcement of the resurrection. We see here as well that the contemplative is not removed from history and does not remain external to history, but becomes the one who is in the heart of history, the one who refers to himself or herself the very heart of things and of happenings. So where the eyes of men and women see only a disfigurement of the human epoch, the eyes of the faith can see reconciliation through the blood of the Son of God, crucified for man. Then the announcement of peace is something beautiful and new, that starts from the fountain of grace poured out through Christ crucified, calling to mind the words of Pascal: 'Christ crucified suffers until the end of the world.'

All this is in the perspective of the proclamation of Easter: this is the vision of the contemplative. Educated in the school of the Word of God, such a person comes to know deeply that the Lord will not allow his saint to see corruption. The Lord will not permit the last word to be said by evil, by sin, or by death, because the contemplative knows that it is exactly there that the Lord will respond to the cry for help that He hears coming from a human person.

Contemplation as the evangelization of the new person

At the root of all conceptions of contemplation there is the transfiguration wrought in a person being conformed to the Word of God. When the Word of God has uplifted us to the point that renders us like him, he is in fact born within us as we come to know the new person that accepts being guided by the Spirit. The root of contemplation is the birth of the new person. But this is the fruit of the patient work of transformation that produces within us a constant and daily encounter with the Word of God. In *Lectio Divina* the baptismal experience is relived by each person, for encounter with the Word of God allows us to descend into the abyss of our own selves. It takes us by the hand and propels us upwards from the bottom that we had touched with sin to emerge into the luminous experience of Easter morning, finally opening in front of us the transcendent space of newness of life in contemplation.

The new person will then be able to utilize new senses: only one who is born in the Holy Spirit will have eyes able to see how, despite everything, history itself is manifesting the mystery of the death and resurrection of Christ. From here springs all the vast grammar and symbolic references of the mystics, speaking of visions, of different tastes, of unexpected conditions, of new and almost tactile perception, of fragrant scents. But common to each sensible human experience will remain the sensitive presence of the Holy Spirit.

Just because they have transformed themselves to the point of seeing everywhere the presence of the Word, of the Logos, contemplatives become the only truly catholic Christian missionaries. In fact only the contemplatives can dedicate themselves to mission: for if this does not follow from transformation by the Spirit, it may occur that, while it claims to bring the good news of the gospel, it brings instead only human words. If mission is not whole in the sense of being one and holy through contemplation, there is not that authority that dwelt in the words of Jesus, but there is simply acting, the cacophony of all our agitating, with the illusion of doing it for the good of the Church and for the glory of God.

The goal of *Lectio Divina* is evangelization; and it is important to determine this last moment of *Lectio Divina*, for the fruit of authentic contemplation is obtained only when the shell of the warm maternal breast is broken open and it allows others to be able to tap into that same Word that has transformed us in our hearts. The arrival point of the Catholic journey is not the closing in of oneself, but the proclamation of the good news of Christ to the world.

Wisdom from Camaldoli

In the thousand-year-old tradition of Camaldoli there have been revealed three progressive steps in the spiritual journey of the Catholic Christian. The first step is constituted by the principle of community life: '*Novitier venientibus de saeculo desiderabile coenobium:* to one who has just started his own journey of conversion, it is appropriate to offer the gymnasium of community life.' There, where the stones can rub against each other and can purify each other, they can also reinforce, build up and construct together until the moment in which a Christian can feel sufficiently strong to continue alone. Then and only then: '*Maturis vero et deum vivum sitientibus aureo solitudo:* to one who is mature and has been captivated by thirst for the living God, the solitary life is pure gold.' He must be able no longer to rely any more on the help that comes from others, because otherwise he would remain a child for eternity. He must start to face the walk of life alone, in solitude. As he progresses, nurtured by encounter with the Word of God, when all other supports have collapsed, be it the person that can always more or less help us, or all the practices that have assisted us until that decisive moment when we encounter personally Christ the Word, then indeed the solitary life is like an unadulterated precious metal, like gold itself.

But this is not enough: once we have reconstructed ourselves as a result of encountering Christ who is the Word of God, and once the Word has become our backbone, our solid point of reference, then the tradition of Camaldoli, starting from St Romuald himself, adds: '*Cupientibus dissolvi et esse cum*

Christo evangelium paganorum: to one who finally has grown to the point of being able to reach the experience of contemplation, and who like St Paul wishes to be completely united with Christ, to him is offered the way of evangelization of the pagans, to him is offered the way of mission.'

In this vision, that is so linear and progressive, there is no place for any opposition between the active and contemplative life: there is only a forward movement. The active life is rather identified with discipline, with *ascesis* or struggle, with the sweated labour that is fulfilled in comprehension not only of the literal sense of the Scriptures, the first step of prayer, but flows into the gift of contemplation, which alone renders us capable of mission, of evangelization, of apostleship, which means being sent forth into the world.

9

The power to forgive

Lectio Divina *on Matthew 9.1–8*

Literal meaning and structure

Let us now search within this text for all the transitions that
we have seen already. First of all we will follow it carefully,
then we will search to discern the structure. There will follow
a meditation that will bring us to the point of prayer. We will
see finally wherein lies the contemplation of this text or an
experience of contemplation arising from it.

So Jesus got into the boat and crossed over, and came to his
own town. Some men appeared, bringing to Jesus a paralysed
man on a bed. When he saw their faith Jesus said to the man,
'Take heart, my son; your sins are forgiven.' At this some of
the scribes said to themselves, 'This man is blaspheming!'
Jesus realized what they were thinking, and said, 'Why do you
harbour evil thoughts? Is it easier to say, "Your sins are
forgiven" or to say, "Stand up and walk"? But to convince you
that the Son of Man has authority on earth to forgive sins' – he
turned to the paralysed man – 'stand up, take your bed, and go
home.' And he got up and went off home. The people were
filled with awe at the sight, and praised God for granting such
authority to men.

Careful reading leads us to distinguish the diverse parts of this story or *pericope*. As we have already seen, sometimes there are some verbal or adverbial expressions, or some conjugation that repeats itself, to mark a subdivision.

The first part of the passage is marked by the first verse: So Jesus got into the boat and crossed over, and came to his own town. The second section starts with verse 2: here there is the famous phrase – *kai idoù*, 'and behold' in English. This part describes the experience of Jesus encountering the faith of those that bring the paralysed man, an encounter that impacts on the problem of the third character, the paralysed man himself.

Another section starts in verse 3, and once again with the phrase – *kai idoù*. It seems incidental because it is about the spectators of the preceding encounter of faith, who formulate the hidden thought: 'this man is blaspheming!' To this hidden thought Jesus answers directly. If there had been no critical and evil spectators, all would have been accomplished by the end of the second section. The argument between Jesus and the scribes allows us to clarify what is the central affirmation of the whole text, contained in verse 6: 'But to convince you that the Son of Man has authority on earth to forgive sins.' This is the heart of the whole story, it is the good news; the gospel of this passage is that the Son of Man has the power to forgive sins on earth. Of such power this healing is a sign, a proof, demonstrating the fact that the paralysed man can be cured inside himself as well as in his body. The theme of the story then is the forgiveness of sins, while the visible miraculous cure is in a way secondary and serves only to corroborate the power of the Lord to forgive sins.

Here then is gathered together the literal meaning of the text. It is already very dense in itself and it casts a different light on the importance of the miracle: the most important thing is not that the paralysed man can walk on his own legs, but that he believes in the forgiveness of his sins, those sins that, according to the biblical tradition, as we have seen, are the root of each evil including physical ones in human life.

Within the literal sense however is indicated the way to approach forgiveness of sins. It is described in the second section of the story in the words: 'When he saw their faith Jesus said . . .' For it is within the journey of faith that we have in some way the guarantee of being able to receive from Jesus as a gift the forgiveness of our sins. There is a further emphasis at the literal level: Jesus answers initially, not to the faith of the paralysed man himself, but to the faith of those who have brought him. It seems that each of us has an assurance of being welcomed by Jesus by virtue of the community of faith that brings us.

Meditation on the Word of God

Let us now attempt to give space to meditation. Immediately the promise of Jesus to his disciples at the end of the Gospel of Matthew should spring to mind: 'Full authority in heaven and earth has been committed to me. Go therefore to all nations and make them my disciples; baptize them in the name of the Father and the Son and the Holy Spirit' (Matthew 28.18–19).

Baptism, from *baptizo*, means being immersed. The command is then to go and immerse all peoples in the name of the Father, of the Son and of the Holy Spirit. Immerse them in the name of Jesus who is the living one, for he is not the God of the dead but of the living and he alone restores life. The *exousia*, the power or authority that Jesus has is received through the Cross: by it he guarantees to each person the possibility of being immersed in the life of the Father and of the Son and of the Holy Spirit, and so to be reborn.

Remaining with the word *exousia*, the power to forgive sins is connected to the faith of the group that brought the paralysed man in front of the Lord. The text of Matthew 18.15–20, which speaks of the redemption from sins within of the Church community, springs now to mind. Let us compare this text with that of our *Lectio Divina*.

At first sight there is a clear mutual responsibility in a Christian community with regard to the forgiveness of deliberate sins, a responsibility from which the community cannot completely withdraw. Thus Matthew 18.15–20, could seem to be a text describing progressive excommunication of a sinner; but in reality is a stimulus to a progressive responsibility on the part of the Church.

'If your brother commits a sin' is evident in the situation of the paralysed man: he is one of the 'little ones' in the gospel, whom Jesus says in Matthew 18.14 that the Father does not want to become lost. How can this be assured to this insignificant person, to this paralysed man, this possibility of receiving the good news of the remission of his sins? The insignificant person is taken on someone's shoulders and he is brought in front of the Lord. If it cannot be done alone, if our faith is not sufficiently robust to be able to support by ourselves the sinful state of this 'little one', then we ask for help from others, perhaps two or three persons who also care. If not even with the help of these two or three can we support the situation, because our faith is so weak that it collapses under the weight of sin, we involve the Church. We take this paralysed person in his little bed together with the whole Church and place him or her in front of the Lord.

Immediately after Matthew 9.8 is presented the encounter between Jesus and the tax-collectors, almost to urge us to trust in the mercy of God those for whom the intervention of the whole Christian community has apparently wrought no benefit, knowing that God is able where we fail. There is then a relationship with the profound sense of faith in the phrase in Matthew 18.17 in relation to considering someone who is unreachable like a pagan and a tax collector, if we compare it with the passage of this *Lectio Divina* in Matthew 9. For it was when he saw their faith that Jesus said to the paralysed man what he did. The faith of the Church is the guarantee, so much so that Jesus returns to it in Matthew 18.19: 'If two of you agree on earth about any request you have to make, that request will be granted by my heavenly Father.'

But it is necessary truly to agree on earth; to love truly is vital, because as long as judgement and penalty exist in place of Christ's justification and there is no space for love, that brother will remain on his little bed and Jesus cannot be described as seeing our faith and being able to say to the paralysed person that their sins are forgiven. The Church then has a huge responsibility: so great that Jesus says in verse 18 of chapter 18: 'Whatever you forbid on earth shall be forbidden in heaven, and whatever you allow on earth shall be allowed in heaven.'

The responsibility with regard to the 'little one' who has committed sin, or towards the paralysed person prostrate on their narrow bed, is so great that it has a value in heaven as well as on earth. Here is the Church, the community that is the paradigm of divine compassion: for Jesus can act only according to their faith.

The power of prayer

Meditation at this point should move into prayer. This must be prayer that is about the Church: 'I believe, Lord; help my unbelief' (Mark 9.24). In the measure by which I see still present in history, through sin, the sign of the wound caused by Satan, I am challenged, with my lack of faith, with my incapacity to love, with my personal inadequacy and that of my friends and of the whole Christian community, that has been called by the Lord to bring this person, this representative of our common humanity, in front of him, so that He can say: 'Your sins are forgiven.'

Our prayer first of all is that of compunction that transforms from within, turning around, upside down and inside out, our detached way of reading these Gospel pages and all the detached ways of evading evil present in the world: I can no longer feel with clean hands for in some way I am, with others, responsible for the sins present in the world.

But if in relation to this plight the Lord promises that if two or three of us will agree on earth to ask any thing, we will obtain it, let us ask then that the Father will increase harmony among us, the reciprocity of human warmth and welcome, until the Lord grants forgiveness on earth as a result of our common prayer.

If then we see that some people awaken, so that there opens to them a vision of life truly renewed, and there are signs of peacefulness and flowering of goodness, we can also think that in the community there is still the faith sufficient for this, and thank the Lord for His goodness which transcends the limits of our senses. We can then progress in prayer, allowing ourselves to become impregnated and transformed by grace, letting us cross from an attitude of complaint and of pessimism in the face of the persistent presence of sin in the world and in each of us, to a universal and truly catholic fellowship – *koinonia*; this witnesses to the beautiful new creation implicit in the truth that the Son of Man has the power on earth to redeem and forgive sins. Then gratitude transforms itself into praise, inasmuch as we open ourselves to the beautiful renewal that comes from the Lord.

Possible directions of contemplation

In the measure by which we, conforming to Christ, become the carriers of this beautiful new reality into the world, we become people able to see the beginning of reconciliation with God in the history of humanity and in the personal history of a person and of a community, in each manifestation of new life present in the world. We become finally at the same defining moment of time's fullness, true contemplatives, missionaries and mystics. As such we give breath to humanity, to the point that, as happened to the paralysed man in the Gospel, regaining newness of life, a person becomes aware that he or she can walk on their own, but not in solitude.

Contemplation and evangelization identify themselves, as when the Apostle Paul says that he no longer lives, but Christ in him (Galatians 2.20). He says as it were that it is no longer my word, but the Word of God, having forever transformed me completely, that is the substance of my message. Truly all has been renounced to follow Christ. There is a perfect conformity to him, for whom we are become Christ-bearers.

'I did not come to call the virtuous, but sinners.' Lectio Divina *on Matthew 9.9–13*

It is said that the most difficult thing when faced by a Gospel passage is the discovery of its structure, of its centre. This is indeed true; it is a difficult operation and exegetes do not always agree among themselves, conjecturing often one or another structure. We must not be afraid. They are all hypotheses: philological science also has to proceed through hypothesis. The exegetes that would give absolute value to their hypotheses are not to be taken too seriously. Obviously a minimal objective reference is necessary, if not, anyone could affirm anything. Important for any definite hypothesis are proofs. These alone can generate assent or dissent among those who examine them, rendering the hypothesis acceptable or not. For it is all about finding a harmonious discourse arising from the whole text.

As we have already seen, there are some signs in the text that help us to discern the structure of the Gospel text. Key verses, as we have said, are often signalled by the particular evangelist with standard phrases, like the adverbs of time and of place: *kai idoù* ('and behold'), *kai egheneto* ('and it happened'), *tote* ('then'), *kai idontes* ('and seeing'). In the Gospel it is also important to distinguish when it is Jesus speaking from the story that is often interwoven around a *logion*, or saying of Jesus, a later oral expression of his teaching or tradition.

To accentuate this process there is also the phenomenon of alliterations, the balance of endings and beginnings, repeated in such a way that the text could almost be sung (for example the Beatitudes), in a kind of chant. This would also serve the purposes of memorization.

Descriptions of movement must also be observed particularly, because they are often needed to connect diverse passages: 'going', 'coming', 'along the road' – all typical expressions of Luke that are often needed also to confer vitality and movement. They are thematically a representation of the journey of the Word of God, as is also evident in the Acts of the Apostles.

Literal meaning and structure

'As he went on from there Jesus saw a man named Matthew at his seat in the custom-house, and said to him, 'Follow me', and Matthew rose and followed him. When Jesus was having a meal in the house, many tax collectors and sinners were seated with him and his disciples. Noticing this, the Pharisees said to his disciples, 'Why is it that your teacher eats with tax collectors and sinners?' Hearing this, he said, 'It is not the healthy who need a doctor, but the sick. Go and learn what this text means, "I require mercy, and not sacrifice." I did not come to call the virtuous but sinners.'

Let us now distinguish the diverse parts of the story. There is clearly a first part found in verse 9. Then verse 10 is introduced by the phrase *kai egheneto*, 'and it happened', which introduces a new section. All that comes before is considered concluded; now there is a different situation.

First of all, however, we notice Jesus walking, and in a moment of time he saw Matthew, a look that like a dart thrown towards a precise point would catch for an instant its objective. The look of Jesus is not a casual look; it is penetrating, acute like a dart. He accompanies it with a concrete command, saying: 'Follow me.' Note, not just 'follow', but also 'follow me.' It is an invitation to an alternative life: so Matthew arose and followed him.

The verb *Anastas* – 'got up', is a word that can be used also for resurrection; it does not mean only 'having stood up', but also perhaps 'reborn': the verb of the resurrection hints at Matthew being 'renewed within'. The result of the sharpened dart that has hit him has caused a turnover in the heart of Matthew. One moment he was seated at the desk of the tax collectors: 'follow me' has meant for him no longer following that which has preoccupied him up till now, for that was symbol of the Mammon of unrighteousness, in which he was held captive by Satan. He has now to choose between two masters once and for all.

This encounter with Jesus has become for Matthew the beginning of a new life: he cannot avoid celebrating it. What has happened to him is very beautiful. He is born anew; he is

THE POWER TO FORGIVE

resurrected. But with whom should he celebrate this event? Surely with his old friends the other tax collectors. In the Gospel of Matthew it is not said that the banquet or the supper was prepared at his house, it is indicated instead in the other evangelists.

The familiar phrase *Kai egheneto* begins the second part of this story with the action described within it. At verse 12 Jesus pronounces his maxim, which is composed of three affirmations in a progressive movement that concludes with the final justification for his approach. The first affirmation asserts: 'It is not the healthy who need a doctor, but the sick.' The second commands: 'Go and learn what this text means, "I require mercy, not sacrifice."'

The first affirmation is in human terms very comprehensible. The second is drawn from Holy Scripture; because the interlocutors of Jesus also believed that in them God spoke. It is like an invitation to study the Scriptures well and to learn their message; indeed to learn and to act accordingly through *Lectio Divina*.

The third affirmation is the conclusive one as if to say: 'Understand, on the grounds of normal human experience, as well as the proof that comes from the Word of God, that I did not come to call the virtuous, but sinners.'

This final affirmation of Jesus we can retain as the heart of the whole story. Seen as such it gives us a kind of depth, in which Matthew's vocation is only a particular example. Or in a reverse manner: what Jesus affirms in the last part of the passage can be considered as justification of the vocation of Matthew. This confirms that the vocation of Matthew is a particular example of the preoccupation of Jesus to cross paths and encounter personally, not those who regard themselves as virtuous, but those who regard themselves to be and who are in fact sinners.

Meditation

If we would want at this point to go on to meditation, making associations and connections we could stop just on the last affirmation of the tripartite answer given by Jesus: 'I did not come to call the virtuous, but sinners.'

Let us concentrate on this text. What does the word 'call' mean? What is meant by the 'virtuous' and the 'sinners'? We could simply reflect on the word 'call', where the verb *kalò*, in the form *kalesai*, as a final infinitive means: 'I came with the purpose of calling.' This means that the coming of Jesus, the coming of the Son of God on earth, is orientated towards the recovery of the sinner. Again more clearly: the very objective of the Incarnation of the Word of God is that of regaining those who were considered lost.

Here we can refer, for example, to the parable of the lost sheep in Matthew 18.12–14 (recalling also Luke's version in Luke 15.1–7) in which the will of the Father is revealed: 'What do you think? Suppose someone has a hundred sheep, and one of them strays, does he not leave the other ninety-nine on the hillside and go in search of the one that strayed? Truly I tell you: if he should find it, he is more delighted over that sheep than over the ninety-nine that did not stray. In the same way, it is not your heavenly Father's will that one of these little ones should be lost.'

This text illuminates the verse that we have proposed above for meditation: for there is more joy over the repentant sinner than over the ninety-nine just ones. In both texts there a reference to the prophecy of Ezekiel, where repeatedly the Lord in the Old Testament tried to make His people understand how much He had in His heart those who were regarded as sinners: 'I myself shall tend my flock, and find them a place to rest, says the Lord God. I shall search for the lost, recover the straggler, bandage the injured, strengthen the sick, leave the healthy and strong to play, and give my flock their proper food' (Ezekiel 34.15–16).

There is an enormous pressure that weighs on those who feel steeped in their sins: they risk ending in desperation. But here is what the prophets say: 'God desires not the death of a sinner but that such a person should turn again to Him and live' (Ezekiel 33.11).

Jesus is then in line with the whole prophetic message in the Old Testament: by confronting the community of Israel he is the one who fulfils the prophetic Scripture. What meaning should be given to the term 'fulfil'? First of all the meaning that speaks of a work completed: the project has been realized. But the word 'fulfil' can also have another meaning, that of putting into action a project: thus Jesus fulfils the prophecies. Further still there is the sense of a dynamic meaning, to 'put into practice'. This is why Jesus sometimes uses the word 'to do': for example, 'the one who does the will of the Father' or 'the one who fulfils the will of the Father'.

We can apply these two meanings to the passage describing the calling of Matthew: Jesus identifies with Matthew and goes to eat with his friends who are regarded as sinners, thus reliving the prophecy of Ezekiel, bringing to perfection the project of divine compassion. According to the other meaning, his action is a deliberate recollection: 'Look, I am putting into practice what was indicated by the prophet Ezekiel.'

Another aspect of 'fulfilment' in the New Testament relates to the concept of fullness, in Greek *pleroma*: A bottle that is full is complete in the sense that it does not lack anything; it does not have any more empty space. There is a kind of totality in something that is fulfilled. This concept is recalled also in the parable of the lost sheep: 'I have ninety-nine sheep on the mountains, I miss that one whose presence is necessary for the fulfilment of the number 'one hundred', which is the total representing fullness or perfection. It is clear that if I want fulfilment in this sense, I want the fullness of my family and I cannot pretend not being aware that one of my children is not at home. Here the term 'fulfilment' has an intense meaning: ninety-nine . . . one hundred! The sinner, or the sinners, in the thought of God are those who are missing from the fullness of His family. In order to give the fullness of Himself to all His children around the same table, He is willing to come down from heaven and to go in active search of the only member who has got lost.

When it is said that in the New Testament and in the Church the Scriptures are being fulfilled until the end of times, we can again apply the threefold meaning of the word 'fulfil'. If we put the accent on the meaning 'end' and see only this, we risk closing to God the possibility of doing new things. It is necessary then to use the word 'fulfil' in order to include the other two meanings, to catch the richness expressed in it.

For two meanings also catch the richness expressed in these words of Jesus: 'I did not come to call the virtuous.' Who are the virtuous? They are those that fulfil the works of justice, which are diligent towards all that the Law prescribes. Jesus takes for granted – and it is very important to note this – that all who follow the Law already belong to the family of God. Who are those that follow the Law? Certainly the Jewish people that are faithful to the Torah or Law of Moses. They are really not excluded at all. To them, however, Jesus recalls the necessity of not keeping their own righteousness enclosed to themselves, but to be open also to those who did not have the capacity to remain faithful to the observance of the Torah of Moses. This call to openness has as its object however not only the sinners among the people of Israel but goes far beyond: for Jesus says elsewhere, 'There are other sheep of mine, not belonging to this fold; I must lead them as well, and they too will listen to my voice. There will then be one flock, one shepherd' (John 10.16).

The Greek word for 'sinners' derives from a verb that indicates the incapacity to attain an objective, to fall short. The virtuous person is then imagined as the one who reaches the objective of the Law, who is faithful to its commandments and so is able to walk on a knife-edge without cutting himself or falling. The sinner, however, is someone whose hand shakes when he throws a dart and so does not hit the target. Jesus invites the virtuous to be compassionate, welcoming, available to those who are not able to walk on the straight road, as they should, to have the same depth of compassion already indicated in the prophecy of Ezekiel. They should not be quick to judge and to condemn someone who has missed the mark, but encourage instead, so that he or she can live. For life is the fulfilment of the Torah personified in Jesus Christ, who said: 'I have come that they may have life, and may have it in all its fullness' (John 10.10).

We can now understand better the sense of the reference to the Scripture: 'Learn what it means: I require mercy, not sacrifice.' The Torah prescribes sacrifice and the righteous person offers it. Jesus however calls the righteous person to be aware that, beyond everything else, that which the Lord expects is mercy. The Greek word for mercy *eleos* has the same root as the word for oil, something that is spread to calm the nerves, to anoint the wounds, to massage the muscles. Oil is also a sign of royalty; it belongs also to the realm of the holy, because it has an invisible energy, an interior strength and warmth. From oil comes scent and scent is the most spiritual symbol that can be imagined: it is perceived by the senses but is not definable and someone who has no perception cannot imagine it even remotely. In this term *eleos* is expressed what is most intimate, something most profound beyond what can be imagined at a human level and that can originate only from God. It is as if he says: 'From you I want that which is behind the term *eleemosyne*, *eleos*: that is, mercy, tenderness, capacity to permeate, to alleviate, to cure, to reinvigorate, to infuse joy back into life.' All of this is therefore intended in the expression: 'I want mercy and not sacrifice. . . . I do not want condemnation with regard to those that have failed, that have not attained the objective, but instead mercy, attention, consideration that is paternal and maternal warmth, the scent of a new life.' This is the oil used by the pre-eminent doctor, Jesus himself.

There comes spontaneously to mind the detail in the story of the Good Samaritan about the oil and the wine (Luke 10.30–37). It is Jesus himself who is the doctor and as such has interest only in the cure of the sick. The doctor is not called to lead a person to the grave, but instead to enable them to be healed, maybe through some very painful experiences. Jesus has come for those that are in need of such a doctor.

This note recurs elsewhere in Luke's Gospel in regard to the virtuous, who, like the Pharisee in the parable (Luke 18.9–14), can too easily put themselves in front of the altar and glorify themselves by their own observance of the Law. In fact it is the sinner, the tax collector – like Matthew – who prays at the farthest end of the Temple and who returns home forgiven and justified: for if he did not reach the mark, God has intervened and has brought him to the point of repentance. From God, the sinner has received the anointing of mercy through the fact that he prayed the words '*kyrie*, *eleison*', a prayer that contains the same term *eleos*. The oil of the goodness and mercy of God has embraced him with its scent.

Epilogue

The mystery of Scripture

There are four senses in Scripture: literal, allegorical, moral, anagogical (or sacramental). A Latin poem, perhaps already known to some readers, puts it thus:

> *Littera gesta docet, quid credas allegoria,*
> *moralis quid agas, quo tendas anagogia*
> The letter teaches the facts;
> The allegory what is necessary to believe;
> The moral what is necessary to do;
> The anagogical points to the goal.

This is a text codified in the Middle Ages, but its substance is much more ancient. Already in the pre-Christian Jewish world the so-called doctrine of the four senses was perceived in the Scriptures; the rabbis embodied it in the Hebrew word *pardesh*, which means 'garden'. Holy Scripture is compared to a garden of delights, the true Eden where men and women can find the food necessary for their journey towards God who is the Highest, and who is beyond us in His transcendence.

The word *pardesh* is formed by four consonants, that in themselves give origin to four diverse Hebrew terms: *pe* to *peshat*, *resh* to *remesh*, *dalet* to *derashah* and *shin* to *shod*.

Peshat indicates the literal sense of the text with which we have already been fully occupied: it is the obligation first of all to understand the literal and historical sense.

Than comes the second sense, the typological, expressed in Hebrew in the word *remesh*, which means 'outline' or 'allusion'. In the Christian tradition, beginning with St Paul, this word is translated normally in Greek by the word *typos* (from which comes typological), which also means *'outline'*, or 'sketch' or also 'scheme': words that come to mind when thinking of the draft of a work of art. It is not yet terminated or completed; however there are already sketched in some way the outlines. Sometimes in Greek another term is also used, *skià*, 'shadow', that points to a reality that projects it. We are as it were in front of a light that shines from behind a reality of which the shadow is the projection. When it is said that Scripture contains the shadow of a definite reality, this is intended to emphasize that the shadow precedes, in some way, our experience of divine reality, which is anyway the true source of the shadow or outline. This is paradoxical and apparently contradictory.

The term *remesh* is also translated in Greek sometimes with the word *eidon*, 'figure'. This describes the figure created by a silhouette projected for example on a wall or on a white surface. There are some surroundings that are precise enough, but the fullness is missing. In this sense one can speak of *eidon* that requires an *eikon*, an image to become more comprehensive. In the image, we have more than a simple shadow, but the image however is not yet the reality. It is an image, for example, that is seen in a mirror: it has all that is necessary for recognition yet it is still only a projection of reality, knowledge of which in a certain sense it anticipates. It makes it tangible; it renders it present to us. The reality is however the *aletheia*, the truth, which is beyond its own image and is that from which the image is projected.

All these words make reference to a reality that precedes them and of which they let us perceive something, permitting us a certain orientation. This orientation, which is concerned with moral behaviour, is expressed by the term *derash* or *derashah*, meaning the moral meaning. We could use a Greek term, the tropological sense, from the word *tropos*, which means 'mode'. Tropology is a model for conduct: seeing the shadow, the figure, the model, we can determine the parameters for our behaviour.

Finally the last meaning, called *shod*, is mystical, that hidden meaning, for in Greek *mystikos* means 'hidden' because it draws from an invisible world, incomprehensible, but real. One enters into this world through an initiation; it is an experience of being drawn into a particular atmosphere, which by definition is ineffable (cf. 2 Corinthians 12.1–10). The mystery is not definable. Many times a person experiences something inexplicable, but still true, being profoundly mindful of it and taken there with both head and heart. Such experiences are near to that which we call 'mystical experience'.

Let us return to the early Christian world, starting with the Apostle St Paul who even before the Evangelists, could not avoid introducing the *typological* vision of the truth recognized in Jesus in application to the sense of the Scriptures. The Old Testament that for the first Christian generation constituted the Scriptures became the book of 'figures' and 'images' of Jesus the Word of God, intimating the mystery of Jesus of Nazareth not yet fully understood. The rock, the stone of the literal sense must be insistently ground until it opens and reveals the mystery of the Word of God, which is Jesus, born in the flesh as the son of Mary. Very often years of reflection are needed, of rumination and meditation, as the fathers would say, to catch in a scriptural text the annunciation of the mystery of Christ. The mystery of Christ is hinted at in the allegorical meaning of the letter.

What is the meaning of allegory? It is a term made of two

Greek words: *allos*, 'other', and *agoreùo* 'propose' and so it can mean 'to speak in public', 'to buy', 'to put out in the market place'. The *agora* (in Latin *ager*) is the open town square as in Siena or Venice. The allegory, then, enables the reader to catch a meaning that is different from that which is public, which is in the market place, that is to say divergent from the literal meaning. However it must be within the letter, not outside its meaning; it is the letter in fact that contains the figure of the truth.

Once discovered under the letter, namely the mystery of the person of Jesus who is the reality that is the origin of the silhouette, we can proceed to search for the moral sense, not before. It is necessary first of all to accept the discipline of the letter, the discipline of the heart, to imbue the process that commits us to search and search, to study and study, to read and reread attentively, until the *mandorla*, the window of heaven opens: then the text will be as it were baptized, purified, and transformed by the death and resurrection of Jesus. Thus we will understand what it means to put it into practice: the following of Jesus, nothing other than that. Any moral reading or spiritual application of Scripture that does not take as its point of reference the discovery of the Christological mystery enshrined in allegory risks becoming simply moralistic reading, even spiritualist, psychological, or sociological; but not spiritual in the full sense of the word.

Remaining close to the mystery of the death and resurrection of Jesus when encountering the Scriptures in their summons to discipleship will induce us to follow Jesus to Calvary and death; and it will mean a transcendence, a continuous movement, rendering ourselves aware that perfection in our comprehension of the text of the Bible consists in the knowledge of never being able to reach it in its fullness. Naturally this is not simply about an intellectual or logical comprehension, but that which involves the integrity of our whole life. This is the goal proposed by Jesus himself: 'Be perfect like your heavenly Father', or 'love others as I have loved you' – goals that no one can pretend to have reached. There is a kind of parallelism between the unfathomable dimension in the meaning of Holy Scripture and the impossibility of each one of us reaching in a complete and definitive mode divine perfection. For this perfection is not only for this life, but also for another eternal life, the constant object of our creative Christian journey. Although having been created within a definite moment of history, the fathers would say, we tend towards the fulfilment of eternity, a fulfilment without fulfilment because God is without limits and we are called to plunge into the self's abyss in Him.

Here we can speak of the mystical sense of Scripture: the unfathomable nature of the anagogic or sacramental meaning in its own mystical milieu. The experience of contemplation makes us aware that there are no words adequate to express it all. If the light shines from on high, if the city is built on the mountain, it becomes a point of reference for all the pilgrims that walk along the valley. If we have an experience of faith, certainly a communication of it will follow. It is useless to worry ourselves about what to say or what to do; it is necessary only to concern ourselves with the Word of God.

The work that we do to descend ever deeper in comprehension of Holy Scripture is parallel to that of rendering ourselves always more open to the Word of God. Then particular exegetical techniques are not in play, but our very lives. You go back to the initial argument: the knowledge of the Scripture is reached through a loving relation, a communion, a fusion with Christ who is the Word of God.

There is no higher knowledge, truer, deeper than that which is established through mutual indwelling. By contrast when a scientist wants to analyse an object, he does so at a distance, to search for 'objective' truth; he is afraid that through any preconception it may not be possible to see the truth of it. This methodology is today far from secure in relation to the Scriptures. In the light of the fathers it is becoming understood even better today that to codify the object of our study in this way is not necessary; it is important instead to relate rightly to it, to become its friends. Only through this friendship or affinity is it possible to discover and understand the secrets of one another, for without love the Scriptures remain a closed book. The path of love is then the path of the following of Christ.

Three levels of human consciousness: body, mind and spirit

There is another way of discerning the progress towards the depths of the sense of the Scriptures. It takes account of that constant in human experience, embracing the three levels of our existential situation: the body, the mind and the spirit.

The fathers teach that the Word of God has been given for the whole human person: in each text of the Scripture we should be able to discover that which the body needs, that which the mind needs and that which the spirit of a person needs, to be included in its integrity. The three levels take in a progressive sense perception, like sequential steps, in which the inferior opens to the superior; so that which the body needs, for example, must not be seen as the only substance of the Holy Scripture, but as a step that allows us to lift ourselves higher and so on.

In the Scripture there are some emphases that refer to the behaviour of the body. Those that are interested only in the body find only these emphases, and they can become negative in an approach that reduces man only to his bodily and physical needs. The letter of the text, comprehended only at this physical level kills because it could lead to idolatry. Expressed as religious legalism it threatens to stifle or even kill the human spirit. Certainly the letter of the text and the body itself are necessary: they are the basis from which we must start. It is absolute bondage to them that distorts and even perverts. The fathers used to say about the Song of Songs (such a lofty text but also so bodily in its language) that if one is inside the world of the senses, reading this text, which is quintessentially mystic and elevated, will be but a carnal experience.

After the level of the body there is that of the mind. When the ancient Greeks spoke of the *psyche* – the mind, they did not intend that which today we identify with the psychological world. The *psyche* was the totality of life, beyond that which is visible, a great part of human experience, but not tangible or physically observable.

For the *psyche* what has been said for the body is also valid. That is: if all our preoccupations are inside the psychic or rational world, intended in the broadest sense, the Scriptures will tell us only things at that level. The risk resurfaces of closing ourselves within apparently relevant intellectual problems, even of idolizing them and of precluding the possibility of coming out of them.

The last level is that of the spirit. Sometimes this is identified with the Greek word *nous*, the intellectual part of the man, or with the *kardia*, the heart, or with the bond existing between the *nous* and the *kardia*, between intellect and heart and the thoughts that circulate between the intellect and the heart. The Word of God – according to the fathers – comprehends even this dynamic goal of our human reality. If inside our hearts there is a reaching out towards the Lord, towards the discovery of the allegory that is Christ himself, then the Scriptures will speak to us of Him.

From all this discussion we have seen how the evidence of the depths of the meaning of the Scriptures is closely connected to our commitment to continuous conversion. If in our lives we pass from the flesh, through the mind, to the spirit, the senses of the Scripture will pass with us from the bodily, through the intellectual, to the spiritual. But if we stall at one of the two first steps, we risk not entering into the world of the Holy Spirit: the text will remain closed before us.

The Scriptures, then, open to men and women in the same measure by which a person is open to the Scriptures. The Word of God reveals himself to a person in the measure by which that person reveals himself or herself to Christ. If the heart is not purified, then the Lord does not open to us, for 'blessed are those whose hearts are pure; they shall see God' (Matthew 5.8). However, as we have also seen, we do not lose the hope that the Lord will remedy what we personally lack through the faith of the Church.

Bibliography

This bibliography is intended to enable those interested in *Lectio Divina* to explore this approach to the Bible further.

Ackroyd, P. R. and C. F. Evans (eds), *The Cambridge History of the Bible*, three volumes, Cambridge University Press, 1970

Bolton, B., *The Rule of St Benedict for Monasteries*, Ealing Abbey, 1969

Bouyer, L., Leclerc, Dom J., and Vandenbroucke, Dom François, *A History of Christian Spirituality*, three volumes, Burns and Oates, 1968

Connolly, S. and O'Reilly, J., *Bede: On the Temple*, Liverpool University Press, 1995

Cousins, E., *Bonaventura – The Soul's Journey into God*, Paulist Press, 1978

Dales, D. J., *Living through Dying: The Spiritual Witness of St Paul*, Lutterworth Press, 1993

Dales, D. J., *Glory: The Spiritual Theology of Michael Ramsey*, Canterbury Press, 2003

Dales, D. J., *A Mind Intent on God: The Prayers and Spiritual Writings of Alcuin*, Canterbury Press, 2004

Dales, D. J., *Glory Descending: Michael Ramsey and His Writings*, Canterbury Press, 2005

Dancy, J., *The Divine Drama: the Old Testament as Literature*, Lutterworth Press, 2001

Danielou, J., H. Musurillo, trans., *From Glory to Glory: Texts from Gregory of Nyssa's Mystical Writings*, St Vladimir's Seminary Press, 1979

Foley, W. T. and Holder, A. G., trans, *Bede: A Biblical Miscellany*, Liverpool University Press, 1999

Gargano, G. I., ed., *Opere di Pier Damiani – Lettere*, Citta Nuova Press, 2000 and forthcoming volumes

Gargano, G. I., ed., *L'eredita spirituale di Gregorio Magno tra Occidente e Oriente*, Gabrielli Editori, 2005

Halporn, J. W. and Vessey, M., eds., *Cassiodorus: Institutions of Divine and Secular learning; On the Soul*, Liverpool University Press, 2004

Hill, E., *St Augustine on Genesis*, Faithworks, 2002

Holder, A. G., *Bede: on the Tabernacle*, Liverpool University Press, 1994

Hurst, D., *Bede's Commentary on the Seven Catholic Epistles*, Cistercian Publications, 1985

Hurst, D., trans, *St Gregory the Great: Forty Gospel Homilies*, Cistercian Publications, 1990

Leclerq, J., *The Love of Learning and the Desire for God*, SPCK, 1978

Malherbe, A. J. and Ferguson, E., trans., *Gregory of Nyssa: The Life of Moses*, HarperSanFransico, 1978

Martin, L. T., trans., *Bede's Commentary on the Acts of the Apostles*, Cistercian Publications, 1989

Martin, L. T. And Hurst, D., *Bede's Homilies on the Gospels*, two volumes, Cistercian Publications, 1991

Matus, T., *The Mystery of Romuald and the Five Brothers*, Source Books, 1994

Matus, T., *Nazarena: An American Anchoress*, Paulist Press, 1998

Moorhead, J., *Gregory the Great*, Routledge, 2005

Oden, T. C., ed., *Ancient Christian Commentary on Scripture*,

series of numerous volumes, Intervarsity Press, 1998–forthcoming

Pelikan, J., *The Christian Tradition – a History of the Development of Doctrine*, five volumes, Phoenix Books, 1971

Schaff, P., ed., *St Augustine's Homilies on the Gospel of St John*, Kessinger Publishing Co, 1974 reprint (Volume VII of 'A Select library of the Nicene and post-Nicene Fathers')

Sperling, H. and Simon, M., trans, *The Zoar*, Soncino Press, 1934

Straw, C., *Gregory the Great: Perfection in Imperfection*, University of California Press, 1988

Smalley, B., *The Study of the Bible in the Middle Ages*, Blackwell, 1952

Temple, W., *Readings in St John's Gospel*, Macmillan, 1945

Vigilucci, L., *Camaldoli: A Journey into its History and Spirituality*, Source Books, 1995

Walsh, K. et al., *St Bernard of Clairvaux: On the Song of Songs*, four volumes, Cistercian Publications, 1976–80

Biblical Index

Old Testament

New Testament

103